25,-

D1307008

Frontispiece: A selection of Scandinavian cheeses; a glazed gammon with vegetables; pieces of eel in a decorative aspic mould; marinated salt herrings; shrimp and lemon smørrebrød.

JYTTE HARDISTY

SCANDINAVIAN
DENMARK/NORWAY/SWEDEN
cooking for pleasure

HAMLYN
LONDON · NEW YORK · SYDNEY · TORONTO

TO JAN AND SANDRA

Published by
THE HAMLYN PUBLISHING GROUP LIMITED
LONDON · NEW YORK · SYDNEY · TORONTO
Hamlyn House, Feltham, Middlesex, England
© Copyright The Hamlyn Publishing Group Limited 1970
ISBN O 600 03648 0
Printed in Czechoslovakia

CONTENTS

INTRODUCTION

It has never to my knowledge been bad manners to talk about food in Scandinavia. On the contrary, what one's friends enjoyed at a dinner party the night before, or indeed are planning to serve at the next one, is a favourite topic of conversation. Since the English in recent times have dropped all pretences and have admitted to finding food an absorbing subject, a great change in eating and cooking habits has taken place, which I have witnessed with great pleasure. Gone are the days when my English friends fried salami and didn't know what Danish pastries were. Smørrebrød and smörgåsbord have become familiar names to most people, and today the Scandinavian cuisine enjoys a reputation which used to be reserved for the French. The three Scandinavian countries—Denmark, Norway and Sweden—which are represented in this book, have for centuries enjoyed a common cultural background and their eating and cooking habits are sufficiently similar to justify a common book on this subject. The three languages are also very similar, though with interesting local variations, as in the case of the recipes. Common to the cooking of all three countries are the two different styles which are to be found: one based on traditional home-grown products, the staple food of everyday family cooking, and the other the rich and succulent party and restaurant food, which is based on the influence of foreign cooking, particularly French. This applies especially to the Danish cuisine, which received its inspiration from France in the 18th century. The first of these styles is represented by the use of cabbage, porridge, thick soups based on pork and cured meat, and fish; the second is represented by elaborate creamy

desserts and cakes as well as by a flair for the art of sauce-making.

In selecting the recipes for this book I have taken three things into consideration: first, the availability of ingredients; secondly, the appeal of the recipes to the English palate; and thirdly my own personal preferences. *Öllebröd*, for example, is ruled out on all three counts. I must crave indulgence from those connoisseurs of Scandinavian food who may search in vain for this and other local specialities. I have also unhesitatingly suggested butter for all cooking and baking purposes, because this is what I prefer. Although recipes must obviously give definite and reasonably accurate proportions of ingredients, I would be the first to admit that most dishes allow room for personal likes and prejudices, particularly in the matter of spices and other flavourings, and some slight deviation from the strict instructions given is perfectly acceptable in many instances. Such latitude, of course, cannot be extended to the main ingredients in baking recipes, where it is important to follow the quantities given in the instructions.

I have attempted to give my readers a fair selection of dishes from each of the three countries, but if Danish cooking seems to have occupied an unfair proportion of the space available, I must be forgiven for being a slightly biased Dane who thinks that there is greater variety to be found in the cooking of her homeland than in that of her neighbours. Finally, I can think of no better title for such a book as this, since cooking is indeed a labour of love in Scandinavia.

JYTTE HARDISTY

EATING THE SCANDINAVIAN WAY

For most people in Scandinavia, the day starts earlier than in England. Work in schools and offices generally begins at 8 o'clock. The early breakfast of coffee or tea and rolls leaves you hungry and ready for the next meal by noon at the latest. It follows that supper must be early as well, usually at 6 o'clock. To fit in with this pattern of meal-times, family life is inevitably different from that in England, particularly at the end of the day. While the harrassed English housewife battles with tea for her hungry children, followed all too soon by supper and bedtime, before she can get down to the preparation of an evening meal for her husband and her exhausted self, her Scandinavian counterpart has only a single meal to prepare. Supper in Scandinavia is a family occasion, and is the main meal of the day for old and young alike. It may consist of soup and a meat or fish course, or a main dish followed by cheese and fresh fruit, or by a simple pudding made from cooked fruit. The rich and luscious sweets are reserved for special occasions and parties, and Scandinavian children do not expect puddings to be a feature of their daily diet.

In Denmark and Norway, one hot meal a day is usually considered enough, and lunch is therefore generally cold, consisting of smørrebrød (open sandwiches). Most workers and schoolchildren take these with them as packed lunches, which they eat in their offices or schoolrooms. The Norwegians, with their practical sense, actually provide Pålæg—various forms of topping such as liver pâté, smoked sausages and cheese—on the breakfast table, where they are made up into sandwiches for lunch, as well as being eaten for breakfast. The Swedes, however,

go in for light cooked lunches, such as omelettes and other egg dishes or Pytt i Panna; Swedish schoolchildren come home for this meal at about 11 o'clock.

Most Scandinavians drink coffee after lunch, or with 'coffee-bread' or biscuits at about 2 o'clock, when it takes the place of English afternoon tea. Afternoon invitations are to coffee, at this time, and provide the chief occasion for eating Danish pastries and other delicious cakes. Dinner parties usually start between 6 and 7 o'clock; drinking before the meal is not a usual Scandinavian habit, particularly when the meal itself is to be accompanied by snaps and beer, and guests are therefore expected to arrive punctually. Do not turn up to a Scandinavian dinner party half an hour late: though this may be considered good form in England, it is enough to drive a Danish hostess frantic while her carefully prepared meal chars in the oven. Other hints on etiquette should include instruction on the convivial drinking ritual: it is not done to raise one's wineglass (or snaps glass) unless one is either saying 'Skål' or responding to this toast; the hum of conversation at a Scandinavian dinner table is punctuated by this word at frequent intervals, from the moment the host proposes the first welcoming Skål. Dry sherry is often served with soup and sweet sherry, Madeira or Port with the dessert. Table wines have long been a feature of Scandinavian entertaining, but certain types of meal call for ice-cold snaps (akvavit) and beer. Chief among these is the typical Scandinavian cold table, but some hot dishes—notably yellow pea soup with pork—also fall into this category.

Any opportunity for a party is welcomed in Scandinavia. Apart from Christmas and birthdays, other annual events, such as Mid-summer Eve, or the start of the crayfish season, regularly provide the excuse for festivity. As much attention is paid on these occasions to the way in which the food is presented at table as to its actual preparation. Meat is carved before it leaves the kitchen and arranged decoratively, surrounded by vegetables, on a serving dish; cold dishes are also prepared with much thought to their appearance—a good hostess will consider the colour combination of her dishes as well as compatibility of flavours and textures.

Hostesses take just as much pride in their table decoration—which should express the mood of the particular occasion—as in the presentation of the food itself. The wide range of beautiful linen and tableware available to them surely stimulates this creative urge in Scandinavian hostesses, and indeed reflects the importance which they attach to this aspect of domestic design. This delight in homely festivity is by no means reserved for parties—even the family supper table will be decorated with candles and informal flower arrangements.

The initials D., N. and S. after each recipe title,
stand for: D. Danish. N. Norwegian. S. Swedish.

KITCHEN EQUIPMENT

There is no need to invest in a lot of new kitchen equipment or tableware before preparing or eating Scandinavian food, but a few items may usefully be obtained if you have not already got them:

1. A cast-iron, enamel-lined casserole with a tightly fitting lid which can be reversed for use as a heavy frying pan or saucepan. Meat and fowl are often roasted on top of the cooker in such a casserole, the oven not being used all that frequently for this purpose. The meat becomes less dry when cooked in this way, and the casserole also provides a practical and attractive way of serving direct from cooker to table.

2. Oblong bread tins, often used for baking cakes instead of round ones.

3. Wooden bowls for salads; boards for cheese and meat; and small individual wooden boards beside each plate for buttering bread, biscuits or crispbread —much easier to manage than on a plate with a raised edge.

4. A good sharp mincing machine, which can tackle raw meat for pâtés and forcemeat.

5. A birch whisk for smooth sauces.

6. A sharp half-moon-shaped chopper—often known by its Italian name of Mezzaluna—is useful for chopping almonds, parsley and many other things.

7. A vegetable slicer, or mandoline.

8. Pestle and mortar for pounding and grinding.

9. Æbleskivepande for Danish doughnuts.

10. Waffle iron for Scandinavian waffles.

11. Ring-shaped mould—an attractive shape for serving a number of sweet as well as savoury dishes.

12. Cheese slicer. Many Scandinavian and other cheeses have a firm smooth texture, and are best cut in thin slices for open sandwiches.

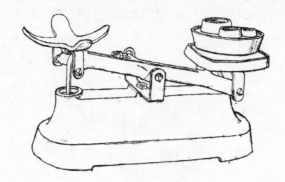

WEIGHTS AND MEASURES

Weights throughout the book are given in lb. and oz. Capacity measure in Imperial pints and fractions thereof, with small amounts in spoon measures. For the benefit of American readers liquid ingredients have been given to the nearest U.S. standard cup measure. These follow the English measure e.g. 1 pint (U.S. $2\frac{1}{2}$ cups).

All spoon measures refer to the British Standards Institution specification. All measures are levelled off to the rim of the spoon. To measure fractions of spoons use the small measures provided in measuring sets or divide the level spoon. The American standard measuring spoons are slightly smaller in capacity than the British standard measuring spoons. The proportion, however, is similar in that 3 American standard teaspoons equal 1 tablespoon.

HANDY CONVERSION TABLE
(Approximate conversion table)

ENGLISH MEASURE		AMERICAN CUPS
1 lb.	Butter or other fat	2 cups
1 lb.	Flour (sifted)	4 cups
1 lb.	Granulated or Castor Sugar	$2\frac{1}{4}$ cups
1 lb.	Icing or Confectioners' Sugar	$3\frac{1}{2}$ cups
1 lb.	Brown (moist) Sugar	$2\frac{1}{4}$ cups
1 lb.	Golden Syrup or Treacle	$1\frac{1}{3}$ cup
1 lb.	Rice	$2\frac{1}{4}$—$2\frac{1}{2}$ cups
1 lb.	Dried Fruit (chopped)	2—$2\frac{1}{2}$ cups
1 lb.	Raw Chopped Meat (finely packed)	2 cups
1 lb.	Lentils or Split Peas	2 cups
1 lb.	Coffee (unground)	$2\frac{1}{2}$ cups
1 lb.	Dry Breadcrumbs	4 cups
8 oz.	Butter or Margarine	1 cup
8 oz.	Lard	1 cup
7 oz.	Castor Sugar	1 cup
7 oz.	Soft Brown Sugar	1 cup (packed)
7 oz.	Candied Fruit	1 cup
$6\frac{1}{3}$ oz.	Chopped Dates	1 cup
6 oz.	Chocolate Pieces	1 cup
5 oz.	Currants	1 cup
$5\frac{1}{2}$ oz.	Cooked Rice	1 cup
$5\frac{3}{4}$ oz.	Seedless Raisins	1 cup
5 oz.	Candied Peel	1 cup
5 oz.	Chopped Mixed Nuts	1 cup

English Measure	Item	American Cups
5 oz.	Sliced Apple	1 cup
4½ oz.	Icing Sugar	1 cup (sifted)
4 oz.	Cheddar Cheese	1 cup (grated)
3½ oz.	Cocoa	1 cup
2½ oz.	Desiccated Coconut	1 cup
2 oz.	Fresh Breadcrumbs	1 cup
1 oz.	Plain Dessert Chocolate	1 square
¼ oz.	Dried Yeast	1 packet
¼ oz.	Gelatine	1 tablespoon
¾ tablespoon	Gelatine	1 envelope
½ oz.	Flour	1 level tablespoon*
1 oz.	Flour	2 level tablespoons
1 oz.	Sugar	1 level tablespoon
½ oz.	Butter	1 level tablespoon smoothed off
1 oz.	Golden Syrup or Treacle	1 level tablespoon
1 oz.	Jam or Jelly	1 level tablespoon

* must be standard U.S. measuring tablespoon

METRIC EQUIVALENTS

It is difficult to convert to metric measures with absolute accuracy, but 1 oz. is equal to approximately 30 grammes, 2 lb. 3 oz. to 1 kilogramme. For liquid measure, approximately 1¾ English pints may be regarded as equal to 1 litre; ½ pint to 3 decilitres (scant); 3½ fluid oz. to 1 decilitre.

OVEN TEMPERATURES

DESCRIPTION OF OVEN	APPROXIMATE TEMPERATURE CENTRE OF OVEN °F	THERMOSTAT SETTING
Very Slow or Very Cool	200—250	¼=240 ½=265 1=290
Slow or Cool	250—300	2=310
Very Moderate	300—350	3=335
Moderate	350—375	4=350
Moderately Hot to Hot	375—400	5=375 6=400
Hot to Very Hot	425—450	7=425
Very Hot	450—500	8=450 9=470

Note THIS TABLE IS AN APPROXIMATE GUIDE ONLY. DIFFERENT MAKES OF COOKER VARY AND IF YOU ARE IN ANY DOUBT ABOUT THE SETTING IT IS AS WELL TO REFER TO THE MANUFACTURER'S TEMPERATURE CHART.

11

A Norwegian smörgåsbord

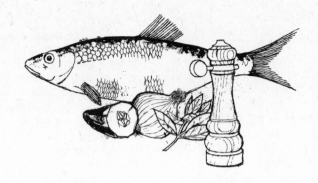

SMÖRGÅSBORD

Smörgåsbord is the Swedish word for the famous Scandinavian buffet table laden with a multitude of different dishes, mainly cold, ranging from spicy cured herrings and other fish, through meats and salads to cheeses. The word literally means bread-and-butter table, the idea being that you help yourself from the various dishes and eat the bread and butter with these. The Danish and Norwegian name is *koldt bord*, which means cold table, but as the Swedish word is internationally better known and sounds nicer I shall use this from now on.

The idea of the smörgåsbord is said to have originated in Sweden at country parties, long ago, when the guests would bring their own dishes and set these out, together with their hostess' contributions, on a large table from which everybody helped themselves. With the shortage of domestic help everywhere, this would seem an excellent way of entertaining nowadays! Unfortunately the old habit died out, leaving the housewife the responsibility of preparing all the food; it is therefore understandable if the giant smörgåsbord, as it used to be known, is disappearing from the domestic scene. It is, however, still the favourite way of entertaining a large number of guests, as a lot of the dishes can be made well in advance, and it remains the traditional family fare on festive occasions such as at Christmas and Easter time.

It is also pleasant to reflect that the giant smörgåsbord is still to be found in many of the big Scandinavian hotels and restaurants, where it is recognised to be a powerful tourist attraction. Lesser versions of the smörgåsbord, on the other hand, are still very popular for a number of different domestic occasions: a selection of herrings as a starter to an ordinary Swedish dinner, or a somewhat wider variety of dishes, including pâtés, salads and cheeses as well as herrings, for an informal luncheon party or late supper.

Whatever the scale of the smörgåsbord, there is quite a ritual attached to it. It is the custom to begin with the various cured herrings; then you change your plate before going on to the salads and meats and—if you have room for it—a small warm dish, before finishing up with the cheese. You should not regard the smörgåsbord as a mixed hors d'oeuvre in the usual English sense of this term! No Scandinavian hostess would like to see her guests scrambling through a mixture of cured herrings, delicate pâtés, mayonnaise salads and cheese, all on the same plate. It is true that a few of the dishes should accompany some of the others (see suggestions below), but give each individual dish a chance to be tested and judged on its own merits and do not feel obliged to ruin your stomach by trying them all.

The following recipes represent a selection of the kind of dishes to be found on a large smörgåsbord, including a few hot dishes. In addition there might be various cold roast joints and fowl as well as a large selection of smoked and cured sausages and cheeses. Various kinds of bread such as Danish rye bread, white bread, Norwegian wafer-thin 'flatbrød' and Swedish 'knäckebröd' (crisp bread) would be served.

Snaps, or akvavit, as it is also called, and beer are the ideal drinks for a proper smörgåsbord. Snaps is usually served in the traditional 'klukflaske' (shown on the frontispiece of this book), so called because of the gurgling sound it makes when you pour from it. Serve the snaps ice-cold in small glasses, which should preferably also have been pre-chilled. Never serve it as an aperitif before a meal: it is essentially a drink to go with food, particularly savoury food like herrings and cheese. You will be further educated in the ritual of snaps-drinking on a visit to Scandinavia, when you will be taught some of the songs which have been written in its praise and to say 'skål', which is the Scandinavian word for 'cheers'.

Now for a few words about the herrings, which are amongst the most popular dishes on the smörgåsbord

13

in all the Scandinavian countries. The herring industry is a flourishing one, thanks not only to the good catches, but also to the ingenious ways in which the herrings are canned in a variety of different sauces such as lobster, wine, dill and tomato sauce. These are often sold abroad under the name of 'gaffelbiter' or 'tidbits'. In addition, salted herrings are used in the home for pickling and marinading in combination with herbs and spices to produce a great many delicious dishes. You will find that all the continental delicatessen shops will stock either salt herrings (whole or filleted) or herrings in brine. These herrings should always be soaked before putting into a marinade, according to the instructions given below in the individual recipes. The third variety, the 'matjes' herring, is probably the best known abroad. It is sometimes sold by weight but more often in cans. These herrings need no previous soaking before using and they may be substituted for the salt herrings in all the herring recipes if desired. Whatever variety of herring is used, the marinade should always be cold when it is poured over them.

MARINATED SALT HERRING

D. MARINERET SILD
N. SPEKESILD
S. INLAGD SILL

Preparation time 15 minutes
To serve 8—12

You will need

8 large salt herring fillets
water *or* milk and water for soaking
14 fl. oz. (U.S. 1½ cups) wine vinegar
7 fl. oz. (U.S. ¾ cups) water
6—7 oz. sugar
1—2 bay leaves
8 whole allspice (optional)
5 whole peppercorns
1—2 onions, sliced

Soak the herring fillets in water, or equal quantities of milk and water, for 8—12 hours.
Remove the fillets, drain and place them in a stone or glass jar. Mix the vinegar, water and sugar and stir until the sugar is dissolved. (Alternatively, boil the water with the sugar and mix it with the vinegar and leave to cool). Add the bay leaves, allspice, peppercorns and onions and pour the cold marinade over the herrings. Cover the jar and leave the herrings in a cold place for 6—12 hours.
When ready to serve, cut the required number of fillets into slices about 1 inch thick, place on a serving dish and garnish with either freshly chopped onions or dill. Serve with thickly buttered dark rye bread and ice-cold snaps and cold lager. Marinated herrings will keep for about 8 days if kept covered, in a cold place. This recipe is a basic one for a number of the following recipes, which introduce many variations (see photograph page 22).

CHEF'S MARINATED HERRING

D. GLARMESTERSILD
N. GLASSMESTERSILD
S. GLASMÄSTARSILL

Preparation time 25 minutes
To serve 6—8

You will need

4 salt herring fillets
water *or* milk and water for soaking
5 allspice, crushed
2 bay leaves
3—4 whole peppercorns
1 small carrot, sliced
small piece horseradish, scraped and sliced
1 large (red) onion, thinly sliced
4 oz. granulated sugar
3 tablespoons water
12 fl. oz. (U.S. 1½ cups) white wine vinegar

Soak the herring fillets in water, or equal quantities of milk and water, for 8—12 hours. Remove the fillets, drain and pack them into a large glass jar with the crushed allspice, bay leaves, peppercorns, carrot, horseradish and onion. Boil the sugar with the water and vinegar. Leave the marinade to cool and, when cold, pour over the herrings. Leave to stand in a cold place for two or three days before serving straight from the jar (see photograph page 20).

MATJES HERRING

These herrings need no soaking before use. Serve them cold, on ice cubes if you like, with hot, boiled new potatoes and cold butter, and with either chopped dill, or with chopped chives and sour cream. Serve beer and ice-cold snaps with this dish.

A Swedish smörgåsbord

MARINATED SALT HERRING WITH HERBS

D. SILD I GRØNT
N. SPEKESILD I GRÖNT
S. SILL PÄ GRÖNT

Preparation time 20 minutes
To serve 4

You will need

2 soaked salt herring fillets (see page 14)
marinade as for marinated salt herring (see page 14)
2 tablespoons finely chopped dill
2 tablespoons finely chopped chives
2 tablespoons finely chopped parsley

Cut the herring fillets into 1-inch pieces and place them in a glass jar. Pour a little of the marinade over the herrings and scatter the chopped dill, chives and parsley into the jar (see photograph page 20).

MARINATED SALT HERRING WITH ONION AND TOMATO

D. LØG OG TOMATSILD
N. SPEKESILD MED LÖK OG TOMAT
S. SILL MED LÖK OCH TOMAT

Preparation time 20 minutes
To serve 4

You will need

2 soaked salt herring fillets (see page 14)
marinade as for marinated salt herrings (see page 14)
1 medium-sized onion, thinly sliced
1 large tomato, thinly sliced
sprigs of dill

Cut the herring fillets into 1-inch pieces and arrange as whole fillets on a flat serving dish. Pour a little of the marinade over the fillets and arrange the sliced onion and tomato in overlapping rows on top. Garnish with sprigs of dill.

MARINATED SALT HERRING WITH CARROT

D. GULERODSILD
N. SPEKESILD MED GULRÖTTER
S. SILL MED MORÖTTER

Preparation time 20 minutes
To serve 4

You will need

2 soaked salt herring fillets (see page 14)
marinade as for marinated salt herrings (see page 14)
1 small carrot, very thinly sliced
½ leek, very thinly sliced
1 small onion, cut into wedges

Cut the herring fillets into 1-inch pieces and arrange as whole fillets on a flat serving dish. Pour a little of the marinade over the fillets and arrange the sliced carrots and leek in rows on top. Place onion wedges around the herring fillets.

MARINATED SALT HERRING WITH ONION

D. LØGSILD
N. SPEKESILD MED LÖK
S. SILL MED LÖK

Preparation time 20 minutes
To serve 4

You will need

2 soaked salt herring fillets (see page 14)
marinade as for marinated salt herrings (see page 14)
¾—1 tablespoon pickled beetroot vinegar (see page 32)
1—2 onions, chopped
sprigs of dill

Cut the herring fillets into 1-inch pieces and arrange as whole fillets on a flat serving dish. Mix a little of the marinade with the beetroot vinegar and pour over the herring fillets. Scatter the chopped onions on top and garnish with sprigs of dill.

MARINATED SALT HERRING WITH BEETROOT

D. RØDBEDESILD
N. SPEKESILD MED RÖDBETER
S. SILL MED RÖDBETOR

Preparation time 20 minutes
To serve 4

You will need

2 soaked salt herring fillets (see page 14)
marinade as for marinated salt herrings (see page 14)
3—4 tablespoons pickled beetroot, chopped (see page 32)
1 medium-sized onion, chopped

Cut the herring fillets into 1-inch pieces and arrange as whole fillets on a flat serving dish. Pour a little of the marinade over the fillets and arrange the chopped beetroot and onion in rows on top.

HERRING IN MUSTARD DRESSING

D. SENNEPSSILD
N. SENNEPSILD
S. SENAPSSILL

Preparation time 25 minutes
To serve 4—6

You will need

3—4 matjes herring
2 tablespoons made mustard
8 tablespoons (U.S. ½ cup) salad oil
8 tablespoons (U.S. ½ cup) single cream
1—2 tablespoons sugar
small piece fresh or pickled cucumber, diced
2 tablespoons chopped chives

Cut the matjes fillets crosswise into 1-inch pieces and place them in a jar. Mix the mustard with the oil and add the cream. Mix in the sugar and the cucumber and stir gently. Pour this mustard dressing over the matjes herrings and scatter the chopped chives on top (see photograph page 20). Serve chilled, either with rye bread or with small new potatoes, boiled and sprinkled with dill and cold butter curls.

SALTED HERRING IN CREAM

D. BONDESILD

Preparation time 20 minutes
To serve 4

You will need

4 salt herring fillets
water *or* milk and water for soaking
1 medium-sized onion, grated
1 large cooking apple, cored and grated
¼ pint (U.S. ⅔ cup) double cream, whipped
2 tablespoons white wine vinegar
2 tablespoons sugar
pinch black pepper
mustard and cress
pinch ground paprika

Soak the herring fillets in water, or equal quantities of milk and water, for 8—12 hours. Remove the fillets, drain, cut them into 1-inch pieces and put them in a serving bowl. Scatter the grated onion and apple over the top. Mix the whipped cream with vinegar, sugar and pepper and cover the herrings with this cream marinade. Garnish with mustard and cress and a sprinkling of paprika.

HERRING IN TOMATO DRESSING

D. TOMATSILD
N. SILD OG TOMAT
S. TOMATSILL

Preparation time 20 minutes
To serve 4—6

You will need

4 matjes herrings
2—3 tablespoons granulated sugar
2 tablespoons water
2 tablespoons wine vinegar
3 tablespoons tomato purée
1 small onion, finely chopped
mustard and cress (optional)

Cut the matjes herrings crosswise into 1-inch pieces and place them in a glass jar. Dissolve the sugar in the water and mix with the vinegar, tomato purée and onion. Pour this tomato dressing over the herrings. Garnish with mustard and cress.

HERRING IN SHERRY

D. SHERRYSILD
N. SHERRYSILD
S. SHERRYSILL

Preparation time 15 minutes
To serve 4—6

You will need

2—3 matjes herring
2—3 tablespoons granulated sugar
4 tablespoons water
2—3 tablespoons wine vinegar
scant ¼ pint (U.S. ½ cup) sherry
1 medium-sized onion, thinly sliced
4—5 white peppercorns, coarsely ground *or*
  crushed
sprigs of dill

Cut the matjes herrings crosswise into 1-inch pieces and place them in a serving dish. Dissolve the sugar in the water, add vinegar and sherry. Pour the liquid over the herrings. Scatter with sliced onion and ground peppercorns. Leave in a cold place for a few hours before serving. Garnish with sprigs of dill (see photograph page 20).

ROLLMOPS

D. ROLLMOPS
N. ROLLMOPS
S. INKOKT STRÖMMING

Preparation time 25 minutes
Cooking time 2—3 minutes
To serve 4—6

You will need

6 fresh herrings, cleaned and boned
1 tablespoon salt
1 teaspoon ground black pepper
pinch ground allspice
3 small onions, finely chopped
2½ oz. granulated sugar
3 bay leaves
2 tablespoons water
scant ½ pint (U.S. 1 cup) wine vinegar

Cut the herrings into fillets and scatter salt, pepper, allspice and chopped onions on each fillet. Roll up the fillets, fasten each with a wooden cocktail stick, and place them in a flameproof casserole with the sugar, bay leaves, water and vinegar. Boil for 2—3 minutes, remove from heat and leave the rollmops

to cool in the marinade. When cold, they are ready for serving. Cooked this way, rollmops will keep in a cold place for 2—3 days.

BIRD'S NEST

D. FUGLEREDE
N. FUGLEREDE
S. FÅGELBO

This is an attractive dish for the smörgåsbord. The first person to help himself from the dish mixes all the ingredients until these are well blended.

Preparation time 10 minutes
To serve 4

You will need

8 anchovy fillets, coarsely chopped
2 tablespoons capers
3 tablespoons cold, cooked, diced potatoes
2 egg yolks
2—3 tablespoons chopped pickled beetroot
  (see page 32)
1—2 tablespoons coarsely, chopped onions

Place two egg cups upside down in the centre of a serving dish. Arrange anchovies, capers and potatoes in successive circles around the cups. Replace the egg cups with two egg yolks, and arrange the chopped beetroot, onions and a few capers around the edge of the dish (see photograph on book jacket).

SOUSED HERRING

D. STEGTE SILD I MARINADE
N. STEKT SILD I MARINADE
S. STEKT INLAGD STRÖMMING

Preparation time 35 minutes
Cooking time 10—12 minutes
To serve 4—6

You will need

4—6 fried herrings (see page 72)
marinade (see recipe for marinated salt
  herring page 14)
1 large onion, sliced
chopped chives

Place the cold fried herrings in a serving dish. Pour the marinade over the herrings and arrange the sliced onion rings and chopped chives on top. Leave in a cool place for several hours before serving.

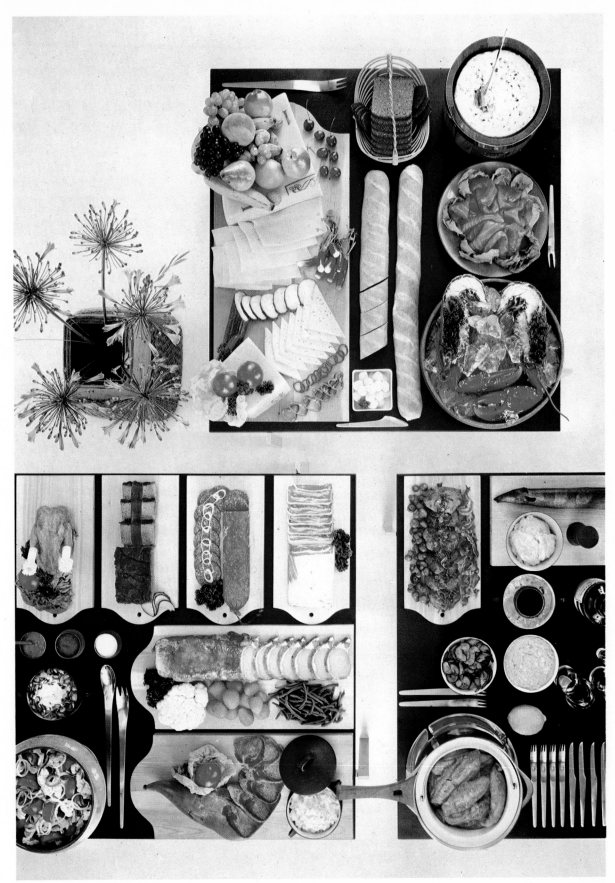

The smörgåsbord

Chef's marinated herring; herring in sherry; herring in mustard dressing and herring with herbs

West Coast salad

21

Some attractive dishes for the Smörgåsbord

HERRING AU GRATIN 1.

N. SILDEGRATENG
S. SILLGRATIN

Preparation time 25 minutes
Cooking time 45—50 minutes
Oven temperature 425°F. Gas Mark 7
To serve 4

You will need

4 fillets salt herring
6 medium-sized raw potatoes, peeled and
    thinly sliced
3 large onions, thinly sliced
ground white pepper to taste
2 oz. butter
brown breadcrumbs

Soak the fillets of salt herring overnight in cold
water and milk. Drain and cut lengthwise. Butter
a shallow baking dish and arrange potatoes, herrings and onions in successive rows. Sprinkle with
pepper and breadcrumbs and dot with butter.
Bake for 45—50 minutes in a hot oven until the
potatoes are cooked. Serve straight from the baking
dish.

VARIATION

The sliced onions may first be sautéed for a few
minutes in butter, without browning them.

HERRING AU GRATIN 2.

D. SILDEGRATIN

Preparation time 25 minutes
Cooking time 20—25 minutes
Oven temperature 375°F. Gas Mark 5
To serve 4

You will need

4 fillets salt herring
1 lb. cooked, cold potatoes, sliced
3 onions, finely chopped
scant ¼ pint (U.S. ½ cup) single cream
1 oz. butter, melted
2 tablespoons brown breadcrumbs
chopped chives

Soak the fillets of salt herring overnight in cold
water and milk. Drain and cut them crosswise into
pieces, 2 inches wide. Place them on the bottom of
a well-greased fireproof dish. Arrange layers of the
sliced potatoes on top and sprinkle with chopped
onions. Pour the cream and melted butter over the
top and sprinkle with breadcrumbs. Bake towards
the top of a fairly hot oven, for 20—25 minutes.
Sprinkle with chopped chives and serve.

HERRING SALAD 1.

D. SILDESALAT

Herring salad in slightly different versions is a
favourite in all three Scandinavian countries.

Preparation time 30 minutes
Cooking time 10 minutes
To serve 4—6

You will need

1 oz. butter
1½ oz. plain flour
scant ½ pint (U.S. 1 cup) stock or milk
6 tablespoons vinegar from pickled beetroot
    (see page 32)
1 teaspoon granulated sugar
1 teaspoon mustard powder
pinch curry powder
pinch pepper
1 medium-sized onion, grated
1 salt herring, cleaned, filleted and
    soaked for 8—12 hours in water
1 cold cooked potoato
1 cooking apple, peeled and cored
4—5 oz. cold, roast or boiled, meat
1 medium-sized pickled beetroot (see page 32)
1 small pickled gherkin
2 tablespoons salad oil
mustard and cress
2 hard-boiled eggs (optional)

Melt the butter over low heat and add the flour.
Cook for 1—2 minutes, then add the stock gradually;
continue cooking over low heat and let the sauce
boil for 3—4 minutes. Stir in the beetroot vinegar,
whisk vigorously and remove the sauce from the
heat. Season with sugar, mustard powder, curry
powder, pepper and grated onion and leave to cool.
Drain the salt herring fillets and cut them cross-.
wise into ½-inch pieces. Dice the potato, apple, meat,
beetroot and gherkin and add all these ingredients
to the red sauce. Toss the salad with two forks so that
all the ingredients are well blended. Leave to stand
for 30 minutes, then stir in the salad oil and pour
the salad into a serving dish. Garnish with mustard
and cress and sliced hard-boiled eggs.

HERRING SALAD 2.

N. SILDESALAT
S. SILLSALLAD

Preparation time 15—20 minutes
To serve 4—6

You will need

2 salt herring fillets, soaked overnight in cold
    water
4 medium-sized boiled potatoes, diced
3 medium-sized pickled beetroots
    (see page 32), diced
1 pickled gherkin, diced
2 medium-sized cooking apples, peeled, cored
    and diced
2 tablespoons chopped onion
salt
pinch pepper

FOR THE DRESSING
beetroot juice (see page 32)
7 tablespoons double cream

TO GARNISH
hard-boiled eggs
chopped parsley

Dice the soaked herring fillets and mix very
thoroughly in a large bowl with all the salad ingredients. Add the seasoning, beetroot juice and
finally the lightly whipped cream. Put the salad
into a bowl or pack it into a mould. Chill thoroughly
and when ready to serve, turn out on to a serving
plate. Garnish with slices or wedges of hard-boiled
eggs or with the yolks and whites chopped separately
and with chopped parsley.

VARIATION
If the cream is omitted the salad may be served
with sour cream.

WEST COAST SALAD

N. VESTKYSTSALAT
S. VÄSTKÜSTSALLAD

This salad was obviously invented to make use of
the delicious shellfish caught off the West coast of
Norway. It is, however, possible to make a tasty
salad from canned shellfish, although it will remain
only second best to the original version. Served in a
large glass bowl, or in individual small ones, it also
makes a feast for the eye (see photograph page 21).

Preparation time 30 minutes
To serve 4—6

You will need

1 large lettuce, cleaned
6—8 oz. cooked lobster meat (fresh or canned)
4—6 oz. cooked mussels (fresh or canned)
4 oz. cooked, peeled shrimps or prawns
4 oz. mushrooms, cleaned and sliced
2 large tomatoes, quartered
4 oz. cooked, fresh or canned asparagus, cut
    into 2-inch pieces (optional)
sprigs of dill

FOR THE DRESSING
1½ tablespoons wine vinegar
5—6 tablespoons olive or salad oil
½ teapoon salt
pinch black pepper
pinch sugar
3 tablespoons chopped dill

Line a glass dish with some of the larger leaves of
the lettuce and shred the remainder. Drain the
lobster meat, mussels and shrimps if canned. Cut
the lobster meat into small pieces and layer in the
glass bowl with the mussels, shrimps, sliced raw
mushrooms, quartered tomatoes, asparagus pieces
and shredded lettuce. Shake the ingredients for the
dressing in a tumbler and pour over the salad. Toss
lightly with two forks and serve cold garnished with
sprigs of dill (see photograph page 21).

FISH SALAD

D. FISKESALAT
N. FISKESALAT
S. FISKSALLAD

Any cooked white fish which is left over from a
previous meal may be used for this salad.

Preparation time 15—20 minutes
To serve 4

You will need

8 oz. cold cooked fish, flaked
1 piece celery, diced
2 pickled beetroots (see page 32)
2 tablespoons capers
scant ¼ pint (U.S. ½ cup) mayonnaise (see
    page 26)
2 hard-boiled eggs, cut into wedges
mustard and cress

Jansson's temptation

Mix the flaked fish with the diced celery. Cut the beetroot into narrow strips and add to the fish with the capers. Stir in the mayonnaise. Pour into a serving bowl and garnish with wedges of hard-boiled eggs and mustard and cress.

JANSSON'S TEMPTATION

S. JANSSON'S FRESTELSE

Who Jansson was—or if indeed he resisted the temptation—I do not know. However, this dish is a classic in Swedish cooking, and the pungent flavour of anchovies, onions and potatoes makes it an excellent dish for the smörgåsbord. The recipe really calls for the Scandinavian type of canned anchovy (sometimes called Marinated Sprats). If this is unobtainable, the smaller Portuguese type may be used, but they should be soaked in milk for an hour or so, to remove some of the salt.

Preparation time 30 minutes
Cooking time 1 hour
Oven temperature 375°F. Gas Mark 5
To serve 4

You will need

2 large onions, thinly sliced
1½ oz. butter
5 medium-sized raw potatoes, peeled and cut
    into thin matchsticks
16 anchovy fillets (24 if using the small
    Portuguese variety)
scant ½ pint (U.S. 1—1¼ cups) single cream

Sauté the onions in ½ oz. of the butter until they are golden and transparent—do not allow them to brown. Remove the onions from the frying pan and layer them, with potatoes and anchovy fillets, in a buttered ovenproof dish, starting and ending with a layer of potatoes. Dot with butter and place in a fairly hot oven for 10 minutes. Pour half the cream over the contents of the dish and return to the oven for a further 10 minutes. Add the remaining cream and cook until the potatoes are soft—about another 40 minutes. Serve at once.

VARIATION
Substitute bucklings for anchovies and you have KARLSSON'S TEMPTATION!

MAYONNAISE

D. MAYONNAISE
N. MAJONES
S. MAJONNÄS

When we talk about mayonnaise in Scandinavian cooking we never refer to salad cream out of a bottle, we mean the real thing—fresh egg mayonnaise, preferably home-made. Some people still seem to consider the making of mayonnaise both laborious and beyond their skill, but there is nothing difficult or magical about it. There are only two important points to remember. One should have all the ingredients at room temperature. The eggs should not come straight out of the 'fridge, nor should the oil and vinegar come straight from a cold larder. The second point is to add oil to begin with, literally drop-by-drop; if it curdles even then, see the remedy given below. Mayonnaise will keep for several weeks if it is covered and stored in a cool place, such as the least cold part of the refrigerator.

Preparation time 10—15 minutes

You will need

2 egg yolks
½ level teaspoon salt
¼ level teaspoon pepper
½—1 tablespoon wine or tarragon vinegar *or* lemon juice
generous ½ pint (U.S. 1¼ cups) olive or salad oil

Stir the egg yolks with the salt and pepper for one minute; add the vinegar and stir. Add the oil drop-by-drop to begin with, stirring all the time. When the mayonnaise begins to thicken, be a little bolder and add the oil in an intermittent thin stream until all the oil has been absorbed. Adjust seasoning to your liking.

NOTE

To thin the mayonnaise: beat in a teaspoon or so of water, thin cream or dry white wine, according to the purpose for which it is to be used.
To lighten the mayonnaise: fold in ⅛—¼ pint (U.S. ⅓—⅔ cup) whipped cream.
To remedy a curdled mayonnaise: add it, very gradually at first, to a fresh egg yolk stirred in a bowl.
Any of the following flavours may be added to the mayonnaise:
tomato purée
mustard
grated horseradish
herbs: chopped dill, parsley, chives or tarragon and chervil.

TARTARE SAUCE

D. REMOULADE
N. REMULADESAUS
S. REMOULADSÅS

Preparation time 30 minutes
To serve 4

You will need

2 tablespoons finely chopped pickled gherkins
2 tablespoons capers
1 small onion, finely chopped
2 tablespoons finely chopped parsley
1 tablespoon finely chopped chervil
1 tablespoon finely chopped tarragon
scant ¼ pint (U.S. ½ cup) mayonnaise
1 tablespoon whipped cream

Add the gherkins, capers, onion, parsley, chervil and tarragon to the mayonnaise and stir. Chill, and immediately before serving, add the whipped cream; stir again and serve with cold roast beef or fried fish.

CURRY SALAD

D. KARRYSALAT

Preparation time 30 minutes
Cooking time 10 minutes
To serve 4—6

You will need

scant ¼ pint (U.S. ½ cup) mayonnaise
1—2 level teaspoons curry powder
2 drops Worcestershire sauce
2 tablespoons whipped cream (optional)
1 salt herring fillet, soaked in water for 6—12 hours then cut into thin strips 1 inch long
2 oz. cold, cooked chicken or veal, cut into thin strips 1 inch long
1 medium-sized gherkin, finely chopped *or* small piece of fresh cucumber, chopped
1—2 hard-boiled eggs
herring tidbits
mustard and cress

Blend the mayonnaise with the curry powder and Worcestershire sauce. Add the cream, if used. Carefully fold in the previously soaked and drained herring fillet, the chicken, gherkin and hard-boiled eggs. Mix well to combine all the ingredients. Pour into a serving dish and garnish with small pieces of

herring tidbits and/or mustard and cress.
In spite of its name, this salad is an old favourite in Danish cooking and is always found on the smörgåsbord, usually served with ham or other cold meat.

SHRIMP SALAD 1.

D. REJESALAT

Preparation time 20—25 minutes
To serve   4—6

You will need

¼ pint (U.S. ½ cup) mayonnaise
½ teaspoon ground paprika
2 tablespoons whipped cream (optional)
8 oz. cooked, peeled shrimps
2 oz. small, cold fish balls, sliced (see page 74)
mustard and cress

Season the mayonnaise with paprika and fold in the cream, if used. Carefully stir in the shrimps and fish balls. Put the salad into a serving dish and garnish with mustard and cress.

SHRIMP SALAD 2.

D. REJESALAT

Preparation time 30 minutes
To serve   4—6

You will need

scant ¼ pint (U.S. ½ cup) mayonnaise
2—3 tablespoons medium-dry sherry
2—3 oz. cooked, peeled shrimps
4—5 oz. mushrooms, trimmed and sliced
5—6 oz. cold cooked asparagus, cut into
  1-inch pieces
mustard and cress

Season the mayonnaise with the sherry. Carefully stir in the shrimps, raw mushrooms and asparagus pieces. Garnish with mustard and cress or, alternatively, with a few extra shrimps.

VARIATIONS

1. Crab or lobster meat may be used instead of shrimps, making it into krabbesalat or hummersalat in Danish.
2. A slightly less rich salad may be made by omitting the mayonnaise and sherry, simply tossing the ingredients in a vinaigrette dressing, and serving the salad on a bed of lettuce, without the mustard and cress.

ITALIAN SALAD

D. ITALIENSK SALAT

Preparation time 10 minutes
To serve   4—6

You will need

scant ¼ pint (U.S. ½ cup) mayonnaise
½ teaspoon mustard powder
½ teaspoon lemon juice
5 oz. cold cooked carrots, cubed
4 oz. cold cooked peas
4 oz. cold cooked asparagus, cut into 1-inch
  pieces
1 oz. cold cooked macaroni, cut into 1-inch
  pieces
mustard and cress
lemon twists

Season the mayonnaise with the mustard and lemon juice. Carefully stir in the cooked carrots, peas, asparagus and macaroni. Pour into a serving dish and garnish with tufts of mustard and cress and lemon twists.

Ham and asparagus rolls

27

HAM AND ASPARAGUS

D. SKINKE OG ASPARGES

Preparation time 10 minutes

Wrap cooked asparagus, fresh or canned, in slices of cooked ham. Place in a serving dish and garnish with halved tomatoes and parsley (see photograph page 27). Serve with Creamed or Dill Butter (see pages 66 and 67).

DANISH COLD POTATO SALAD

D. KOLD KARTOFFELSALAT

Preparation time 20 minutes
To serve 4

You will need

scant ¼ pint (U.S. ½ cup) mayonnaise
pinch curry powder
chopped chives, parsley or dill
2 lb. cold, cooked potatoes, sliced
2 small shallots or onions, chopped

Season the mayonnaise with curry powder and chopped chives, parsley or dill and carefully fold the potatoes and onions into it. Scatter with chopped chives. Chill, and serve with cold roast meat, ham, hard-boiled eggs or Salt Duck or Goose (see page 102).

Swedish hot dog and potatoes

COLD POTATO SALAD

N. POTETSALAT
S. POTATISSALLAD

Preparation time 25 minutes
To serve 4

You will need

6—8 medium-sized lukewarm cooked
    potatoes, peeled and sliced or diced
garlic
2 tablespoons finely chopped parsley, chervil
    and tarragon *or* 2—3 tablespoons finely
    chopped pickled beetroot (see page 32)
1—2 tablespoons capers
1—2 tablespoons chopped chives

FOR THE DRESSING
1½—2 tablespoons wine vinegar
5—6 tablespoons olive or salad oil
1 teaspoon salt
¼ teaspoon ground white pepper

FOR THE GARNISH
capers
chopped beetroot
finely sliced leek or chopped chives or parsley

Arrange the sliced potatoes in a serving bowl which has been rubbed with a clove of garlic. Sprinkle the parsley, chervil and tarragon and beetroot on top and add capers and chives. Mix the vinegar, oil, salt and pepper in a tumbler and shake the dressing well, before pouring it over the ingredients in the bowl. Leave the potato salad to stand in a cold place for several hours. Just before serving, garnish with capers, chopped beetroot and either sliced raw leek, chopped chives or parsley.

GRATED CARROT SALAD

D. REVNE GULERØDDER

To serve 4

Peel 1 lb. carrots (old carrots have more flavour than new ones) and grate them. Children like them with a sweetened lemon juice dressing and sprinkled with parsley. Serve them on the smörgåsbord mixed with a vinaigrette dressing, flavoured with a touch of garlic (see page 67) and decorate with parsley, chives, dill, chervil or tarragon. This is surely one of the easiest, cheapest and most delicious salads.

MEAT JELLY (ASPIC)

D. SKY

Dark brown meat jelly is used in Scandinavian cooking on the smörgåsbord, accompanying liver pâté, amongst other things. It is also cut into small strips or squares and used as garnish for smørrebrød (see page 35). Meat jelly used to be made by boiling beef or veal bones for 5—6 hours, after these had been browned first in fat with the addition of browned vegetables and herbs. As time seems so precious to all of us nowadays, few people have the patience or the inclination to spend too long in the kitchen when they can use certain short cuts in cooking. Various alternatives for making good tasty meat jellies are therefore used today.

Canned bouillon, canned consommé or, though not so good, beef bouillon cubes may be turned into meat jelly by adding unflavoured gelatine in the proportions of 8—10 thin leaves of gelatine to each pint liquid, or gelatine powder (see recipe for Scandinavian Rice Pudding, page 125, for proportions). Soy or gravy browning may be added for colouring and a tablespoon of Port, Madeira or brandy for flavouring; the wine or brandy should be added to the hot stock after the gelatine has been dissolved. As most of the alcohol will evaporate, this small amount of liquid will not upset the proportion of gelatine.

LIVER PÂTÉ 1.

D. LEVERPOSTEJ
N. LEVERPOSTEI
S. LEVERPASTEJ

Liver pâté is a regular feature of the Scandinavian diet. It comes in many forms: the texture can be rough or smooth and it can either be a simple pâté or it can be enriched with cream and truffles for special occasions. The Scandinavian pâtés differ from most French pâtés in that they do not, as a rule, contain either garlic or wine and their texture is, on the whole, more soufflé-like than the French. There are a multitude of recipes from which to choose, but the two below are good examples, one for daily use and one for special occasions. Pig's liver is excellent for pâtés, but calf's liver is perhaps even better, though unfortunately more expensive. If you use calf's liver the pâté will usually have a more attractive pink hue than if it is made with pig's liver. If you have a very obliging butcher, perhaps

he will mince the liver, pork and fat for you. In that case, you only need to put the liver mixture through your own mincer once; alternatively, if you have no mincer, chop the rest of the ingredients finely before adding them to the meat mixture. An electric blender can also be used successfully.

Preparation time 1 hour
Cooking time 1½ hours
Oven temperature 325—350°F. Gas Mark 3—4
To serve 8—10

You will need

9 oz. pig's or calf's liver
9 oz. fillet or other lean cut of pork
9 oz. pork fat
1 medium-sized onion, quartered
3 large anchovy fillets
   or 1 salt herring fillet
1½ oz. butter
1½ oz. plain flour
½ pint (U.S. 1¼ cups) milk
1 egg
pinch salt
pinch ground black pepper
¼ teaspoon ground cloves
¼ teaspoon ground allspice

Wipe the liver with a damp cloth and dry. Cut the liver, pork and pork fat into small pieces. Render down a little of the pork fat in the oven, in an oblong mould or tin (a 2 lb. loaf tin is ideal), so as to coat the bottom and sides of the tin with a thin layer of fat. Put the cut liver, pork, remaining pork fat, onion and anchovies through a mincer 3—6 times according to how fine a texture you like your pâté to have. Melt the butter in a saucepan and add the flour. Cook over low heat for 1—2 minutes before gradually adding the milk. Stir all the time and continue cooking until the mixture is thick and smooth. Add the minced liver mixture and stir. Remove from the heat and stir in the egg and spices. Pour into the fat-lined tin and place this in a baking pan with hot water to reach two-thirds of the way up the tin. Bake for about 1½ hours in a warm to moderate oven.

Test if the liver pâté is done by plunging a metal skewer into the centre of the pâté and checking to see if it comes out clean. If you like a nice brown crust on top of the pâté, remove the water-filled baking pan from the oven for the last 15 minutes and bake the pâté on its own for this time. Leave the pâté to cool down in the tin before serving it on the smörgåsbord with mustard and cress, button mushrooms and meat jelly or with pickled beetroot, and cucumber salad (see pages 32 and 30).

LIVER PÂTÉ 2.

D. LEVERPOSTEJ
N. LEVERPOSTEI
S. LEVERPASTEJ

Preparation time 45 minutes
Cooking time 1 hour
Oven temperature 350°F. Gas Mark 4
To serve 8—10

You will need

1 lb. 2 oz. calf's or pig's liver
9 oz. hard back fat of pork
1 small onion
5 anchovy fillets
4 tablespoons plain flour
7 fl. oz. (U.S. ¾ cup and 2 tablespoons)
    double or single cream *or* equal quantities
    of double cream and milk
2 eggs
large pinch ground black pepper
large pinch salt
½ teaspoon ground paprika
½ teaspoon ground cloves
¼ teaspoon ground allspice
2—3 coarsely chopped fresh or canned truffles
    (optional)

Wipe the liver with a damp cloth, dry and cut it into small pieces. Cut one-third of the pork fat into very thin slices and line the bottom of a buttered, 2-lb. loaf tin. Cut the remaining pork fat into small pieces and put these, together with the liver, onion and anchovy fillets, through a mincer 5 times (unless your butcher will do this for you). If an even finer-textured paté is wanted, rub the mixture through a sieve. Stir in the flour, cream, eggs, seasoning and spices. Add the truffles at this stage, if desired. Pour the liver mixture into the buttered loaf tin, place in a baking pan with hot water to reach two-thirds of the way up the tin, and bake in a moderate oven for about 1 hour. Test to see if the paté is done by plunging a metal skewer into the centre of it and check if the skewer comes out clean. Leave the paté to cool down in the tin. Serve with either pickled beetroot or cucumber salad (see pages 32 and 30).

CUCUMBER SALAD

D. AGURKESALAT
N. AGURKSALAT
S. INLAGD GURKA

This easily prepared cucumber salad is usually a great favourite among foreign visitors to Scandinavia. It is the 'salting' process which makes it different from most other cucumber salads. 1—2 tablespoons of oil may be added to the dressing, but this is not the rule.

Preparation time 10 minutes
To serve 4—6

You will need

1 cucumber
salt
scant ¼ pint (U.S. ½ cup) water
½ teaspoon salt
pinch white pepper
scant ¼ pint (U.S. ½ cup) white wine vinegar
    or juice of 1 lemon
sugar to taste (about 3 tablespoons)
2 tablespoons chopped parsley *or* dill

Wash the cucumber and slice it very finely, using a vegetable slicer, if available, so that the slices are almost transparent. Place in a deep bowl and sprinkle with salt. Cover with a plate and weigh down with a heavy object. Leave to stand for 1—2 hours. Drain thoroughly, rinse off the salt and squeeze out the remaining juice. Boil the water and add the salt and pepper, leave to cool and add the vinegar and sugar. When the dressing is cold, pour it over the cucumber and leave to chill for half an hour. Just before serving sprinkle with chopped parsley or dill. Serve cucumber salad with roast chicken (see photograph page 97) or any other roast meat.

BEEF TARTARE

D. BØF TARTAR
N. TARTARBIFF
S. RÅBIFF

Only prime cuts of beef should be used for this dish, which is much favoured in Scandinavian as well as in Dutch cooking. The beef can be served on its own or on pieces of buttered ryebread.

Preparation time 10—15 minutes
To serve 4

You will need

1¼—1½ lb. boneless lean beef (sirloin or fillet)
1 onion, coarsely chopped
capers
horseradish shavings
4 egg yolks

With a very sharp knife scrape the tender raw beef along the muscle fibres. Divide equally into four portions and shape these into flat rounds or squares. Arrange the beef on a flat serving dish and garnish with the chopped onion, capers and horseradish shavings. Place the egg yolks alongside, standing in the halved shells on a bed of coarse salt. Serve at once perhaps with ryebread and butter, but certainly with cold beer.

ROLLED VEAL SAUSAGE

D. RULLEPØLSE
N. RULLESYLTE
S. RULLSYLTA

Preparation time 30—40 minutes
Cooking time 2—2½ hours

You will need

4 lb. lean boned breast of veal (in 1 piece)
1 lb. hard back fat of pork
2 teaspoons salt
1 teaspoon saltpetre
1 teaspoon ground white pepper
1 teaspoon ground cloves
½ teaspoon ground allspice
½ teaspoon sugar
4 tablespoons finely chopped parsley *or* dill
1 tablespoon finely chopped shallot (optional)

Trim the meat into a large square. Arrange the pork fat, cut into thin slices, on two-thirds of the veal and scatter with salt and saltpetre, spices, sugar, herbs and shallot. The meat trimmings may be put on top of the sliced pork fat. Roll up sausage-fashion, from the side where the pork is covering the veal, and tie securely with string. Put the rolled breast of veal into a saucepan and cover with water. Bring to the boil, skim and add seasoning. Cover with a lid and simmer for 2—2½ hours. Place the rolled veal between two plates and put a heavy weight on top. (In the old days a special rolled veal press was used for this purpose, (see photograph). Leave the rolled veal in a cold place for about 10 hours. If it is to be kept longer than a few days it should be soaked in brine. To each 1¾ pints water add 4 oz. coarse salt and 1 tablespoon sugar. Mix the water, salt and sugar and bring to the boil, skim and leave the brine to cool. Submerge the rolled veal in the brine and leave for 3—6 days.
Serve this rolled veal sausage thinly sliced on the smörgåsbord or on smørrebrød (see page 35).

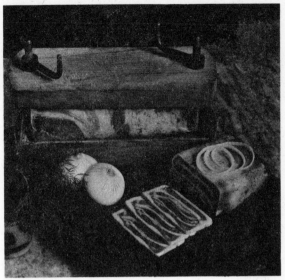
Rolled veal sausage

VARIATION
Breast of lamb may also be used in this way, but omit the back fat of pork.

HAM CONES

D. SKINKE KRÆMMERHUSE

Preparation time 10 minutes

Shape thinly sliced ham into cones and fill these with Horseradish Cream Salad (see page 33). Garnish with a quartered tomato and mustard and cress, or with liver pâté stirred with a little double cream, and piped into the ham cones and garnished with a stuffed olive.

TONGUE SALAD

D. TUNGE SALAT

Preparation time 20 minutes

Arrange sliced, cooked tongue, cooked French beans, halved Smiling Eggs, sliced pickled beetroot (see pages 52 and 32) in successive rows on a serving dish. Garnish with lettuce. Serve Vinaigrette dressing separately (see page 67).

BRAWN

D. SYLTE
N. PERSESYLTE
S. PRESSYLTA

This dish is traditional Christmas fare in Scandinavia. It is no use attempting to make it if you feel squeamish about cleaning the pig's head!

Preparation time 1 hour
Cooking time 2—3 hours
To serve 8

You will need

1 pig's head
2 lb. shoulder of pork
water
salt
4—5 bay leaves
½ teaspoon ground cloves
1 teaspoon ground black pepper
¼ teaspoon ground allspice
¼ teaspoon curry powder

Clean the pig's head and singe off hair and bristles. Clean teeth with a stiff brush and remove the eyes and ears. Soak the head in salted water overnight. Place the pig's head in a saucepan, cover with cold water and add a good pinch of salt and the bay-leaves. Bring slowly to the boil and remove any scum which forms. After 1 hour, add the shoulder of pork and continue cooking for a further 1—2 hours, until the meat is tender enough to fall from the bones. Remove the meat from the soup and leave the soup to cool. Meanwhile, cut all the meat from the bones and cut into small cubes. Place the cubes, alternating lean and fat meat, in a deep bowl, scattering the ground cloves, pepper, allspice and curry between the layers. When the bowl is almost full, top up with a little of the soup. Put a plate on top and weight it down with a heavy object, and leave the brawn in a cool place to set. When ready, turn out on to a serving dish and serve with pickled beetroot (see below), mustard and dark rye bread. Serve ice-cold snaps and lager with this dish.

PICKLED BEETROOT

D. SYLTEDE RØDBEDER
N. SYLTEDE RØDBETER
S. INLAGDA RÖDBETOR

Sweet-sour pickled beetroots often accompany hot meat dishes. They are also found on the smörgåsbord or cold table, together with jellied pork and veal, head cheese, brawn or a variety of other meat dishes, particularly those made from pork, as well as liver pâté.

Preparation time 25 minutes
Cooking time 1½ hours
To serve 8

You will need

1 lb. beetroot
salt to taste
¾ pint (U.S. 1¾ cups) white or red wine
  vinegar
½ pint (U.S. 1¼ cups) water
6 oz. granulated sugar
1 dessertspoon whole cloves
small pieces of scraped horseradish

Wash the beetroot and cut off the leaves. Place beetroot in boiling, salted water and cook for about 1 hour, depending on the size. When tender, drain, cool and peel. Cut beetroot into thin slices and place in glass jars. Mix the vinegar, water and sugar in a saucepan and bring to the boil. Pour at once over the sliced beetroot, add some whole cloves and a piece of horseradish to each jar. Cover with greaseproof paper. (The horseradish prevents mould forming on top of the beetroot). Pickled beetroot will keep in a cold place for about 3 weeks.

SWEDISH FRANKFURTER AND POTATO SALAD

S. KORV-OCH POTATISSALLAD

Preparation time 15—20 minutes
To serve 4

You will need

4—6 lukewarm boiled potatoes, diced
8 oz. frankfurter sausages, sliced
double quantity onion or tomato dressing
  (see page 68)
1 pickled beetroot (see above), diced
2 tablespoons chopped chives

Arrange the potatoes and sausages in layers in a bowl. Pour the dressing over and sprinkle with beetroot and chives. Chill the salad before serving.
Note
The potatoes will absorb the dressing better while still warm. This improves the salad.

HORSERADISH CREAM SALAD

D. PEBERRODSSALAT

Preparation time 15 minutes
To serve 4

You will need

1—2 tablespoons sugar
1—2 tablespoons lemon juice or vinegar
1—2 tablespoons peeled and grated
   horseradish
¼ pint (U.S. ⅔ cup) double cream, whipped
2 oz. cooked macaroni, cut into 1-inch pieces
mustard and cress
ground paprika

Stir the sugar and lemon juice together. Add the grated horseradish to this mixture and stir. Fold in the whipped cream. Add the cooked macaroni pieces and arrange in a serving bowl. Decorate with tufts of mustard and cress and sprinkle ground paprika over the top. Serve this salad with roast beef, ham or chicken; it looks pretty if served in hollowed-out tomatoes. It is also often used as garnish for Danish open sandwiches.

VARIATION
1½ oz. chopped ham may be added to the salad, in which case use only 1 oz. cooked macaroni.

DUCK AND GOOSE DRIPPING

D. ANDE OG GÅSEFEDT
N. ANDFETT OG GÅSFETT

Duck and goose dripping tend to be too liquid to spread on bread, so to remedy this it is usual to blend equal quantities with pork dripping. The spicy dripping below is delicious eaten on dark rye bread with coarse sea salt, salami or other continental sausage, or with smoked meat.

Preparation time 15 minutes
Cooking time 20 minutes

You will need

duck or goose dripping
pork dripping
onion, chopped or finely sliced
grated apple
1 teaspoon salt for each pound of dripping
fresh or dried thyme

Heat the duck or goose dripping with the pork dripping and add the onion, grated apple, salt and thyme. Cook over low heat but do not brown the onion. Pour into a serving dish to set.

SWEDISH HOT DOG AND POTATOES

S. HOT DOG OCH POTATIS

Preparation time 10—15 minutes
Cooking time 8 minutes
To serve 4

You will need

knob of butter
1 small onion, chopped
8 oz. frankfurters, sliced
1½ lb. cold, boiled new potatoes, sliced
2 tablespoons tomato purée
¼ pint (U.S. ⅔ cup) single or double cream
salt
pepper
pinch cayenne pepper
chopped chives or parsley

Melt the butter in a saucepan over medium heat. Sauté the onion until golden and add the sliced frankfurters. Lower the heat and cook for a few minutes. Add the sliced potatoes together with the tomato purée and cream. Cover the pan and cook until heated through. Season with salt, pepper and cayenne. Serve at once sprinkled with chopped chives or parsley (see photograph, page 28).

A selection of Danish open sandwiches

SMØRREBRØD

English-speaking people often confuse the Danish word *Smørrebrød* with the similar-sounding Swedish word *Smörgåsbord*. Whereas the latter means buffet table, Smørrebrød is merely the word for open sandwiches. These form part of the staple diet in all three Scandinavian countries, but especially in Denmark, where most people eat them regularly for lunch. Danes often give a smørrebrød party as an alternative to a smörgåsbord party. This way of entertaining is much more economical of space, though not necessarily of time. The Danes have perfected the art of making smørrebrød to such a degree that the word 'Danish' usually prefaces 'open sandwiches' whenever these are mentioned. This makes such a large mouthful, in more than one sense, that some enterprising person has thought of abbreviating it to 'Danwiches'.

Smørrebrød literally means buttered bread, but this is clearly something of an understatement, for in contrast to English sandwiches, the bread itself usually forms the least conspicuous part, being largely hidden by the topping, which catches the eye at the first glance. Smørrebrød is obviously made to suit each individual occasion—sandwiches made for a quick lunch, to take to school or to the office, are not on the same elaborate scale as those for special occasions, for which a knife and fork are required. Whatever the occasion though, all smørrebrød deserves to be prepared attractively and with attention to detail.

A good open sandwich is a skilful blend of different food flavours, textures and colours, all of which add up to make it a dish in itself. It consists of a half slice of bread, not too thick, buttered not too thinly, a generous topping and a carefully chosen garnish. For certain occasions smaller versions may be prepared: *snitter* in which the bread is cut diagonally to half the usual size, for a midnight snack to wind up an evening's entertainment or for afternoon tea; *canapés*, still smaller and often cut in fancy shapes, as an hors d'oeuvre; and *pindemadder*, literally pin-food, each a single mouthful to accompany cocktails. The last two varieties may be spread with either different flavoured butters or mayonnaise.

As with any other food preparation, it is convenient to put out all the ingredients before you begin to make sandwiches on a large scale. Choose fresh bread with a close texture, preferably Danish rye bread, which is the ideal base for a savoury sandwich. Do not confuse this with the German pumpernickel, which is even darker and good for cheeses, but not for fish and meat on account of its rather sweet flavour. Some of the milder cheeses and pâtés, as well as shellfish and salmon, are best served on white or light brown bread, though this must naturally remain a matter of individual taste.

Spread the butter, and cover with the topping: this may consist of any of the dishes which you find on the Smörgåsbord, but of course any household larder or 'fridge may yield a variety of foods which you can use. If sliced roast meat, ham, smoked salmon or sliced sausages are used, these can be rolled up, folded or layered, to add height to the sandwich. Most of the Danish cheeses are sliced and may be used in the same way. A piece of lettuce is often used under the topping, to prevent moisture from making the bread soggy, but also to add further height to the sandwich as well as providing a crisp, green freshness.

The garnishes which finish off the sandwich should harmonise with the flavour of the meat, salad or fish which make up the topping, as well as adding colour to enhance its appetising appearance. You may choose from a variety of garnishes to suit your own palate. But be guided by this, rather than by the palette! Too often a travesty of Danish open sandwiches is created by the use of a selection of completely inappropriate trimmings, chosen merely for the sake of a spectacular show of colour. Such thoroughly unsuitable garnishes include glacé cherries, and most fresh or canned fruit, all of which belong in fruit salads and not in perverse association with the sturdy flavour of meat and cheeses. You should aim for a fresh gay effect, rather than an ornate or overloaded one. Garnishes may include such colourful items as a simple, pale green lettuce leaf, darker green parsley, chives and dill, pink radishes, bright red tomatoes, wine-coloured pickled beetroots, shavings of pure white horseradish, yellow lemon wedges and ochre-coloured pickles. Under the preparation of individual sandwiches in this chapter, you will find many more suggestions, but the following are a few examples of some of the more unusual ones—unusual that is to foreigners to Scandinavia—with descriptions of how to prepare some of them.

Sandwiches are obviously best eaten when freshly made, but if a large quantity have to be prepared in advance, it is better either to butter the bread, cover it and have all the toppings and garnishes ready in plastic bags to arrange finally, or to make the sandwiches all but ready, except for the garnishes, and cover them lightly with foil or clean, slightly damp tea towels. Leave the half-prepared sandwiches in a cool place until ready to serve and add the garnishes at the last minute.

Serve the sandwiches attractively on flat trays or dishes with perhaps a little more greenery such as parsley or lettuce tucked in between, but don't over-do it—you don't want the finished result to look like a vegetable garden.

In all the following recipes, except where otherwise stated, Danish rye bread or a good coarse brown bread is recommended. The recipes in this section represent some of the most popular varieties, but the possibilities for variation are much greater and some restaurants in Copenhagen boast hundreds of different pieces of smørrebrød on their menus. Choosing from the enormous list of tempting suggestions and subsequently enjoying eating the smørrebrød on a summer's eve, in one of the restaurants in the delightful gardens of 'Tivoli', is for many people one of the most treasured memories of a visit to Denmark.

The order of eating is the same as with the smörgås-bord. Start with the herring varieties and work your way through to the cheeses, but you may want to take short cuts, for you will find that 2—3 pieces of the elaborate kind of smørrebrød will satisfy even the heartiest appetite. Beer and ice-cold snaps are the appropriate drinks to accompany smørrebrød, although tea is often served instead for a late serving of *snitter*.

The following garnishes may be novel ideas to many readers, but they are some of the most commonly used on Scandinavian sandwiches. They are quite easy to make and by their different shapes they add a visual interest to the sandwiches:

Chopped dill, or sprigs of dill Use the leaves, not the crowns of the dill which are used for pickling purposes.

Raw onions Chopped or cut into rings. Use the rings in graduated sizes, two or three interlocking, or use singly to enclose another garnish, for instance, a raw egg yolk.

Tomatoes and red or green peppers Cut in the same way and used after de-seeding.

Lemon twists Cut lemon into very thin slices, then cut each slice from the centre to the outer edge. Twist the ends in opposite directions so that the twist will stand upright.

Cucumber, beetroot, pickled gherkin and tomato Make into twists as above.

Gherkin fans Slice each gherkin lengthwise, almost to the base. Carefully spread the slices out into a fan shape.

Radish roses Top and tail the radishes, but leave a small leaf on each radish, then cut each one from the tip to within ¼ inch of the base. Make two or three similar cuts, diagonally. Put the radishes into ice-cold water for 30 minutes to open out.

Olive spirals Using a small sharp knife, pare each olive crosswise, starting at the top, in a thin continuous strip close to the stone.

Mayonnaise, plain or flavoured Pipe into swirls, rosettes etc.

Cooked prunes Serve with sliced pork, roast duck and goose.

Preparing egg and tomato open sandwich

Egg and tomato open sandwich, ready to serve

EGG AND ANCHOVY

ÆG OG ANSJOSER

You will need

raw egg yolk
anchovy fillets
raw onion ring
capers

Place anchovy fillets on buttered bread leaving a space in the middle for a raw onion ring. Carefully place a raw egg yolk inside the onion ring and scatter a few capers on top of it.

EGG, ANCHOVY AND CAPERS

ÆG ANSJOSER OG KAPERS

You will need

sliced hard-boiled egg
anchovy fillets
capers
chopped raw onion

Place overlapping slices of hard-boiled egg in rows, on buttered bread. Arrange anchovy fillets diagonally over the top and scatter with capers and chopped onion.

EGG AND TOMATO

ÆG OG TOMAT

You will need

sliced hard-boiled egg
sliced tomato
mustard and cress *or* chopped chives

Place overlapping slices of egg and tomato alternately, in rows, on buttered bread. Garnish with mustard and cress or chopped chives.

CHOPPED EGG AND HERRING

HAKKET ÆG OG SILD

You will need

chopped hard-boiled egg
herring tidbits or chopped matjes herring
sprig of watercress

Mix the chopped egg with the herring tidbits and spread on buttered bread. Garnish with a sprig of watercress.

TOMATO AND HERRING

TOMAT OG SILD

You will need

sliced tomato
herring tidbits *or* anchovy fillets
capers
chopped raw onion *or* sprigs of dill

Place overlapping slices of tomato on buttered bread. Arrange herring tidbits in diagonal lines on top. Scatter with capers and raw onion or dill.

SMOKED BUCKLING AND SCRAMBLED EGG

RØGET SILD MED RØRÆG

You will need

smoked buckling, skinned and filleted
scrambled egg *or*
    savoury egg custard (see page 51)
chopped chives

Place alternate rows of buckling and scrambled egg on buttered bread. Scatter chopped chives on top.

SMOKED EEL AND LEMON

RØGET ÅL OG CITRONSKIVE

You will need

smoked eel, skinned and filleted
lemon wedge

Place fillets of smoked eel lengthwise on a piece of buttered bread, to cover it completely. Garnish with a lemon twist.

SARDINE AND LEMON

SARDIN OG CITRONSKIVE

You will need

lettuce
sardines (in oil or tomato sauce)
lemon wedge

Place a small piece of crisp lettuce on buttered bread. Arrange sardines on top and garnish with a wedge of lemon.

SMOKED EEL AND SCRAMBLED EGG

RØGET ÅL MED RØRÆG

You will need

smoked eel, skinned and filleted
scrambled egg *or*
    savoury egg custard (see page 51)
chopped chives

Place fillets of smoked eel lengthwise on a piece of buttered bread, to cover it completely, with a row of either scrambled egg or savoury egg custard alongside. Scatter chopped chives on top.

SMOKED SALMON AND SCRAMBLED EGG

RØGET LAKS OG RØRÆG

You will need

white bread and butter
smoked salmon
scrambled egg *or*
    savoury egg custard (see page 51)
sprigs of dill

Cover a piece of buttered, white bread with smoked salmon, top with scrambled egg or savoury egg custard. Garnish with sprigs of dill.

MARINATED HERRING

SPEGESILD

You will need

marinated salt herring (see page 14)
raw onion rings
sprigs of dill (optional)

Drain the marinated herring, cut it into 1-inch pieces and place them on buttered bread. Arrange overlapping raw onion rings on top and garnish with a sprig of dill.

Danish open sandwiches

A typical after-theatre supper

SHRIMPS AND LEMON

REJER MED CITRONSKIVE

You will need

white bread and butter
lettuce
peeled shrimps
lemon twist
freshly ground black pepper

Top a slice of white buttered bread with a small piece of crisp lettuce. Pile shrimps on to the lettuce and garnish with a lemon twist. Sprinkle with freshly ground pepper (see photograph page 2).

SHRIMPS AND TARTARE SAUCE

REJER OG REMOULADE

You will need

white bread and butter
peeled shrimps
lettuce
tartare sauce (see page 26)
mustard and cress

Follow the instructions for the previous recipe but garnish with a teaspoonful of tartare sauce and a tuft of mustard and cress instead of lemon.

FILLET OF PLAICE AND TARTARE SAUCE

FISKEFILLET OG REMOULADE

You will need

small fried fillet of plaice (cold or warm)
tartare sauce (see page 26)
lemon twist

If serving the fried fillet of plaice cold put it on buttered bread and garnish with tartare sauce and a twist of lemon.
If the fish is warm, serve the buttered bread and tartare sauce separately.

ROAST PORK AND RED CABBAGE

FLÆSKESTEG OG RØDKÅL

You will need

sliced cold roast pork
cold cooked red cabbage (see page 109)
cold cooked prunes
crackling

Place several overlapping layers of thinly sliced roast pork, on buttered bread. Garnish with cold red cabbage, prunes and a piece of crackling.

ROAST PORK, PICKLED GHERKIN AND BEETROOT

FLÆSKESTEG, AGURK OG RØDBEDE

You will need

cold sliced roast pork
sliced pickled gherkin
sliced pickled beetroot (see page 32)

Place several layers of thinly sliced roast pork on buttered bread. Garnish with sliced, pickled gherkin and beetroot.

ROAST LAMB AND CUCUMBER SALAD

LAMMESTEG OG AGURKESALAT

You will need

lettuce
sliced cold roast lamb
cucumber salad (see page 30)
sprigs of dill *or*
   chopped chives

Place a small piece of crisp lettuce on buttered bread. Arrange several layers of thinly sliced roast lamb on top. Garnish with drained cucumber salad and scatter with sprigs of dill or chopped chives.

Preparations for smoked buckling and raw egg yolk

Smoked buckling and raw egg yolk

RISSOLES AND CUCUMBER SALAD

FRIKADELLER OG AGURKESALAT

You will need

lettuce
sliced meat rissoles (see page 92)
cucumber salad (see page 30)

Place a small crisp piece of lettuce on buttered bread and arrange overlapping layers of sliced rissoles to cover it. Drain the cucumber salad and top rissoles with it.

SMOKED BUCKLING AND RAW EGG YOLK

RØGET SILD OG RAA ÆGGEBLOMME

You will need

smoked buckling, skinned and filleted
sliced radishes
chopped chives
raw egg yolk
salt

Arrange fillets of smoked buckling on buttered bread. Scatter with sliced radishes and chopped chives and carefully place the raw egg yolk on top. Sprinkle with coarse sea salt.

BEEF TARTARE

BØF TARTAR

You will need

beef tartare (see page 30)
raw onion ring
raw yolk of egg
capers
grated horseradish

Shape the beef tartare to fit the slice of buttered bread. Place a raw onion ring in the centre and carefully slip the raw egg yolk into it. Garnish with capers and grated horseradish.

ROAST BEEF AND TARTARE SAUCE

ROASTBEEF OG REMOULADE

You will need

lettuce
sliced cold rare roast beef
tartare sauce (see page 26)
crisply fried onion rings

Place a small piece of crisp lettuce on a piece of buttered bread. Arrange several layers of thinly sliced roast beef on top. Garnish with a dessert-spoonful of tartare sauce and some crisply fried onion rings.

ROLLED VEAL SAUSAGE AND ASPIC

RULLEPØLSE OG SKY

You will need

dripping (see page 33)
rolled veal sausage, sliced (see page 31)
meat aspic (see page 29)
mustard and cress

Spread a piece of bread with dripping and arrange the sliced veal in overlapping layers. Garnish with a small piece of meat aspic and a sprig of mustard and cress.

ROAST BEEF AND HORSERADISH

ROASTBEEF OG PEBERROD

You will need

lettuce
sliced cold rare roast beef
freshly grated horseradish
pickles *or* glazed onions (see page 110)

Place a small piece of crisp lettuce on buttered bread. Arrange several layers of thinly sliced roast beef on top. Garnish with coarsely grated horseradish and pickles or glazed onions.

ROAST BEEF AND HORSERADISH CREAM SALAD

ROASTBEEF OG FLØDE PEBERRODSSALAT

You will need

lettuce
sliced cold rare beef
horseradish cream salad (see page 33)
watercress *or* mustard and cress
quartered tomato

Place a small piece of crisp lettuce on buttered bread. Arrange several layers of the tinly sliced roast beef on top. Garnish with watercress and tomato wedges.

Preparing ingredients for Danish open sandwiches

LIVER PÂTÉ AND CUCUMBER

LEVERPOSTEJ OG AGURK

You will need

liver pâté
fresh cucumber twist
pickled beetroot (see page 32)
diced meat aspic (see page 29)

Spread the liver pâté fairly thickly on buttered bread or, alternatively, cut it into slices and place these to overlap slightly, on the buttered bread. Garnish with cucumber, beetroot, cut into matchstick-sized strips and parsley (see photograph, page 45).

LIVER PÂTÉ, MUSHROOMS AND BACON

LEVERPOSTEJ, CHAMPIGNON OG BACON

You will need

liver pâté
mushrooms, sautéed in butter
grilled streaky bacon

Follow the instructions for the previous recipe but garnish with a few sautéed mushrooms and a piece of grilled bacon (see photograph, page 45).

Preparation of sliced salami

TONGUE AND ITALIAN SALAD

TUNGE OG ITALIENSK SALAT

You will need

lettuce
sliced cold ox tongue
Italian salad (see page 27)
mustard and cress

Place a small piece of crisp lettuce on a piece of buttered bread. Arrange slices of tongue on top and garnish with a dessertspoonful of Italian salad and mustard and cress.

SALAMI, ONION AND ASPIC

SPEGEPØLSE, LØG OG SKY

You will need

sliced salami
raw onion rings
diced meat aspic (see page 29)

Spread a slice of bread with butter or dripping and arrange overlapping slices of salami over the top. Garnish with raw onion rings, overlapping, a sprig of parsley and a small piece of meat aspic.

Salami, onion and aspic

TONGUE, OLIVE AND ASPIC

TUNGE, OLIVEN OG SKY

You will need

lettuce
sliced cold ox tongue
olive, cut spiral fashion
meat aspic (see page 29)
watercress

Place a small piece of crisp lettuce on buttered bread. Arrange sliced tongue on top. Garnish with a spiral-cut olive and a sprig of watercress.

ROAST SPRING CHICKEN AND CUCUMBER SALAD

KYLLING OG AGURKESALAT

You will need

lettuce
thinly sliced cold roast chicken
cucumber salad (see page 30)
sprigs of dill *or* chopped parsley

Put a small piece of crisp lettuce on buttered bread. Arrange the sliced chicken on top, in several layers. Garnish with well-drained cucumber salad and a sprig of dill.

PICKLED GOOSE OR DUCK AND HORSERADISH CREAM SAUCE

SPRÆNGT GÅS ELLER AND OG FLØDE PEBERRODSSAUCE

You will need

lettuce
thinly sliced pickled goose or duck
horseradish cream sauce (see page 68)
glazed onions (see page 110)
watercress

Place a small piece of crisp lettuce on buttered bread. Arrange the sliced pickled goose on top and garnish with a dessertspoonful of horseradish cream sauce and a sprig of watercress.

Preparation of ingredients for open sandwiches

Liver pâté and cucumber

Liver pâté, mushrooms and bacon

45

Preparing cod's roe

Cod's roe to serve with tartare sauce

COD'S ROE AND TARTARE SAUCE

TORSKEROGN OG REMOULADE

You will need

cold fried cod's roe, sliced (see page 73)
twist of lemon
sprig of parsley
tartare sauce (see page 26)

Arrange overlapping rows of sliced cod's roe on buttered bread. Garnish with a lemon twist and a sprig of parsley. Serve with tartare sauce.

FILLET OF PORK AND MUSHROOMS

MØRBRAD OG CHAMPIGNON

You will need

lettuce
sliced fillet of pork (see page 81)
mushrooms, sautéed in butter
watercress

Place a small piece of crisp lettuce on buttered bread. Arrange sliced fillet of pork on top and garnish with sautéed mushrooms and a sprig of watercress.

SHRIMP SALAD

REJESALAT

You will need

white bread and butter
lettuce
shrimp salad (see page 27)
mustard and cress

Place a small piece of crisp lettuce on buttered white bread. Pile the shrimp salad on top and garnish with mustard and cress.

HAM AND HORSERADISH CREAM SALAD

SKINKE OG PEBERRODSSALAT

You will need

lettuce
sliced ham
horseradish cream salad (see page 33)
quartered tomato
mustard and cress

Place a small piece of crisp lettuce on buttered bread. Arrange sliced ham on top and garnish with a dessertspoonful of horseradish cream salad, quartered tomato and mustard and cress.

Preparing ham, scrambled egg and asparagus

Ham and asparagus

HAM AND ASPARAGUS

SKINKE OG ASPARGES

You will need

lettuce
sliced ham
2—3 small asparagus spears or heads
tomato *or* red pepper ring
sprig of parsley

Place a small piece of crisp lettuce on buttered bread. Arrange sliced ham on top and garnish with asparagus, held in a tomato ring, and a sprig of parsley.

HAM AND SCRAMBLED EGG

SKINKE OG RØRÆG

You will need

sliced ham
scrambled egg *or*
   savoury egg custard (see page 51)
chopped chives

Arrange overlapping layers of sliced ham on buttered bread. Garnish with scrambled egg or savoury custard and chopped chives.

DANISH BLUE WITH BRANDY AND NUTS

D. DANDBLU MED COGNAC OG NØDDER

You will need

Danish Blue cheese
brandy to taste
white bread and butter
coarsely chopped walnuts

Mix Danish Blue with a little brandy until smooth. Spread the mixture on buttered bread and scatter chopped walnuts on top.

Ham and scrambled egg

47

A typical Danish lunch

HERRING SALAD

SILDESALAT

You will need

lettuce
herring salad (see pages 23 and 24)
mustard and cress

Place a small piece of crisp lettuce on buttered bread. Pile the herring salad on top and garnish with mustard and cress.

CURRY SALAD

KARRYSALAT

You will need

lettuce
curry salad (see page 26)
herring tidbits
sliced hard-boiled egg
chopped chives

Place a small piece of crisp lettuce on buttered bread. Pile curry salad on top and garnish with 1—2 herring tidbits and a slice of hard-boiled egg. Scatter chopped chives on top.

ITALIAN SALAD

ITALIENSK SALAT

You will need

white bread and butter
lettuce
Italian salad (see page 27)
mustard and cress

Place a small piece of crisp lettuce on buttered white bread. Pile Italian salad on top and garnish with mustard and cress.

CUCUMBER, TOMATO AND ONIONS

D. AGURK' TOMAT OG LØG

You will need

sliced cucumber
sliced tomato
chopped raw onion

Place overlapping slices of cucumber and tomato in rows on buttered bread and garnish with chopped onion.

48

POTATO AND CHIVES

KARTOFLER OG PURLØG

You will need

lettuce
cold, cooked new potatoes, sliced
chopped chives *or* dill
seasoning
French mustard

Place a small piece of crisp lettuce on buttered bread. Arrange sliced potatoes in overlapping rows along the bread. Scatter chopped chives or dill on top and season with freshly ground black pepper, coarse salt and a dash of French mustard.

CHEESE AND RADISHES

OST OG RADISER

You will need

buttered white bread *or* pumpernickel
sliced Danish cheese
radish rose

Put a generous amount of sliced cheese, in overlapping rows, on buttered bread and garnish with a radish rose.

CAVIAR AND LEMON

KAVIAR OG CITRON

You will need

Russian or Danish caviar
sliced lemon

Spread caviar on lightly toasted buttered rye bread. Garnish with sliced lemon and serve at once.

MATJES HERRING, APPLE AND BEETROOT

D. MATJESSILD MED ÆBLE OG RØDBEDE

You will need

matjes herring
finely grated apple
pickled beetroot (see page 32), cut into thin strips

Cut the matjes herring into 1-inch pieces and place these on buttered bread. Scatter grated apple and pickled beetroot over the top.

Fish soufflé with shrimp and asparagus sauce

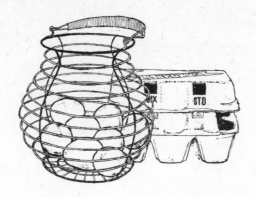

EGG DISHES

Boiled eggs may be found on the Scandinavian breakfast table, but never bacon and eggs, nor indeed any other egg dishes. These are all reserved for luncheon or light supper menus. Fried eggs in a Madeira sauce may be a novel idea to many readers, but is a good old Danish dish served at lunch in restaurants. Eggs, of course, appear in many forms on the smörgåsbord and as part of the toppings for smørrebrød, including raw egg yolks. This seems an appropriate point at which to tackle this vexed question: some of those who are unfamiliar with raw egg yolks on the table seem to feel that they are a danger to health, or perhaps aesthetically unattractive. But they look no different from soft-boiled yolks, and as for their safety, how often have you come to harm from eating them in the form of mayonnaise? Omelettes as the French make them are popular of course, but the Scandinavians also have different versions which contain a little flour or potato flour and in which pork or bacon may be incorporated. Another popular egg dish is thin savoury pancakes, stuffed and rolled with creamed spinach, chopped ham or mushrooms, covered with a sauce béchamel or mornay and cooked *au gratin*. Funnily enough, the Danes talk of *gratin*, when they really mean savoury soufflés such as those described in this chapter.

SAVOURY EGG CUSTARD

D. ÆGGESTAND
N. EGGESTAND
S. ÄGGSTANNING

This savoury egg custard is sometimes wrongly considered by visitors to Scandinavia to be merely a form of scrambled egg. While scrambled egg is also made in Scandinavia, savoury egg custard is often used in its place on open sandwiches instead, as it does not make the bread soggy, and it looks rather more elegant. Savoury egg custard is also used, cut into small cubes or fancy shapes, as garnish for soups or cooked fish. Meat or vegetables may be added to the custard to make luncheon dishes or hors d'oeuvre. It can also be baked in a pastry flan case (see photograph page 55).

Preparation time 10 minutes
Cooking time 20—30 minutes
Oven temperature 325°F. Gas Mark 3

You will need

4 eggs
7 fl. oz. (U.S. ¾ cup and 2 tablespoons) single cream *or* milk
good pinch pepper
1 teaspoon salt
nutmeg (optional)

Beat the eggs lightly and add the cream or milk. Season with pepper, salt and perhaps a pinch of nutmeg. Pass the egg and milk mixture through a sieve a couple of times. Butter a shallow dish and pour the custard mixture into this. Cover with a piece of greaseproof paper or a lid and stand on a rack in a pan of hot water with the water reaching only three quarters of the way up the dish. Bake in a warm oven for 20—30 minutes until firm. The custard is ready when a knife plunged into the centre comes out clean. Make sure the custard does not boil, or it will be full of holes. Leave to cool a little, before turning out of the mould.

SMILING EGGS

D. OVERSKÅRNE ÆG or SHILENDE ÆG

These are what the French call Oeufs Mollet. Gently boil standard eggs for 5 minutes and large eggs for 6—7 minutes. Place them in cold water and carefully remove the shells after cracking gently all over with the back of a spoon. Keep the shelled eggs submerged in warm water if it is to be served hot, or in cold water if it is to be served cold. The eggs are halved lengthwise with a sharp knife. In Scandinavian cooking they are often used in such dishes as Mock Turtle and also in soups like Chervil Soup (see pages 84 and 62).

SPINACH RING

D. SPINATRAND
N. SPINATRAND
S. ÄGGSTANNING MED SPENAT

Preparation time 10 minutes
Cooking time 35 minutes
Oven temperature 325°F. Gas Mark 3
To serve 4

You will need

1 lb. fresh spinach, washed
4 large eggs
scant $\frac{3}{4}$ pint (U.S. $1\frac{3}{4}$ cups) single cream or milk
$\frac{1}{2}$ teaspoon salt
pinch ground white pepper
pinch nutmeg

Pour boiling water over the spinach, drain and chop it finely. Beat the eggs lightly and add the cream or milk. Season with salt, pepper and nutmeg, add the chopped spinach and stir. Butter a ring-shaped mould and pour the spinach custard mixture into it. Stand the mould on a rack in a pan of hot water with the water reaching only three quarters of the way up the dish. Bake in a warm oven for 35 minutes until firm. The dish is ready when a knife plunged into the centre comes out clean. Make sure the custard does not boil, or it will be full of holes. Loosen all round the edge with a knife and carefully turn out on to a serving dish. Serve either hot or cold. The centre of the mould may be filled with either creamed sweetbread or shrimp and asparagus sauce (see pages 94 and 69). The latter makes a very attractive colour combination with the spinach ring.

Note
Chopped, frozen spinach may be used, but it should only be thawed and drained before mixing with the eggs and cream.

PORK OMELETTE

D. FLÆSKEÆGGEKAGE

Preparation time 15 minutes
Cooking time 18 minutes
To serve 4—6

You will need

12 oz. streaky pork, thinly sliced
4—6 eggs
2 tablespoons potato flour (optional)
generous $\frac{1}{4}$ pint (U.S. $\frac{3}{4}$ cup) milk
salt
pepper
chopped chives
quartered tomatoes

Fry the sliced pork until it is golden brown. Remove from frying pan and pour off half the fat drippings. Beat the eggs with the potato flour, milk, salt and pepper, then pour this egg mixture into the frying pan. Arrange the sliced pork and tomatoes on top of the egg mixture and cook the omelette over low heat for about 10 minutes, lifting its edges from time to time with a palette knife. This allows the uncooked egg mixture to run underneath. Cook until the omelette is set, but still moist on top. Scatter with chopped chives. Serve straight from the frying pan with butter, dark rye bread and your favourite mustard (see photograph page 53).

VARIATION
Sliced bacon may be used instead of streaky pork.

OVEN OMELETTE

N. OVNSOMELETT
S. UGNSOMELETT

Preparation time 5 minutes
Cooking time 25—30 minutes
Oven temperature 350—400°F. Gas Mark 4—6
To serve 4

Pork omelette

You will need

4 eggs
½ pint (U.S. 1¼ cups) single cream
salt
ground pepper

Lightly beat the eggs with the cream and seasoning.
Melt a little fat in a flameproof dish measuring 6—7
inches in diameter and pour in the egg mixture.
Cook the omelette in a moderate to fairly hot oven
for 25—30 minutes until lightly brown. Loosen the
edges of the omelette and serve it either directly
from the dish in which it was cooked or on a hot
serving dish. Serve with a filling of either creamed
mushrooms, creamed sweetbreads, creamed kidneys
or shrimp and asparagus sauce (see pages 110, 94,
and 69). Pour the filling over half the omelette and
fold over the other half. Serve at once.

VARIATION

A cheaper version of the omelette may be made by
using only 3 eggs, 1 tablespoon plain flour, salt,
pinch pepper and ¾ pint (U.S. 1¾ cups) milk.

BAKED HAM PANCAKE

N. FLESKEPANNEKAKE I
OVN S. FLÄSKPANNKAKA

This could be described as a Scandinavian 'toad in
the hole' and is an excellent way of using the last of
a joint of ham.

Preparation time 10—15 minutes
Cooking time   30—40 minutes
Oven temperature 435°F. Gas Mark 7
To serve   4

You will need

2 eggs
1 pint (U.S. 2½ cups) milk
6 oz. plain flour
½ teaspoon salt
pinch pepper
8—12 oz. slightly salted or smoked ham or
   bacon

Whisk the eggs with a little of the milk, add the
flour and whisk to a smooth batter. Add the remainder of the milk and stir in the seasoning. Leave
the batter for 10—15 minutes. Meanwhile, cut the
ham or bacon into small cubes and fry these lightly
in a small baking or roasting tin measuring about
8 by 12 inches. Pour the batter over the ham and
bake in a hot oven for 30—40 minutes until the pancake is set and browned. Serve with cranberries.
Note
Chopped chives may be scattered over the pancake
after it has been removed from the oven.

SMOKED BUCKLING OMELETTE

D. BORNHOLM OMELET

The best Danish smoked bucklings come from the Baltic island of Bornholm. If you ever manage to find them, try a freshly-smoked buckling which is still warm and sprinkle it with coarse salt. You will never find a better delicacy.

Preparation time 25 minutes
Cooking time 10 minutes
To serve 4

You will need

3 small smoked buckling
6 large eggs
8 tablespoons (U.S. ½ cup) milk
1 level teaspoon potato flour *or* cornflour
pinch pepper
butter
sliced radishes
chopped chives
2 medium-sized tomatoes, quartered

Remove the heads, skin and bones from the buckling. Beat the eggs with the milk and potato or cornflour and season with pepper. Melt some butter in a frying pan and pour the omelette mixture into the pan. Cook over low heat, lifting the edges of the omelette to allow the uncooked egg mixture to run underneath. When the omelette is beginning to set, but still moist on top, place the buckling fillets in a star shape on top. Put sliced radishes in a pile in the centre and place quartered tomatoes around the edge of the omelette. Finally, sprinkle chopped chives over the top and serve hot, straight from the pan (see photograph page 85). Serve a fresh green salad or watercress with the omelette.

EGGS IN MUSTARD SAUCE

D. SKIDDENÆG

This is a traditional Danish Easter dish which may be found amongst the small dishes on the Smørgasbord.

Preparation time 10 minutes
Cooking time 8 minutes
To serve 4

You will need

1 portion mustard sauce (see page 69)
pinch nutmeg
4 large eggs

Make the Mustard Sauce using dark French mustard for preference and season with a little nutmeg. Boil the eggs as for 'Smiling Eggs' (see page 52); shell them while they are still warm and place them in a deep dish. Pour the hot Mustard Sauce over the eggs and serve at once with French bread.

Smiling eggs used as a garnish for Mock Turtle

POACHED EGGS AND SPINACH

D. SLØRAEG OG SPINAT
S. FÖRLORADE ÄGG MED
SPENAT

Preparation time 15-20 minutes
Cooking time 15-20 minutes
To serve 4

You will need

4 poached eggs
4 pieces hot toast
thin slivers smoked salmon, optional
1 portion creamed spinach (see page 109)

Arrange the poached eggs on the pieces of toast and garnish each egg with slivers of smoked salmon. Pour the hot creamed spinach around each piece of toast and serve at once.

EGGS IN MADEIRA SAUCE

D. SPEJLAEG I MADEIRASKY

Preparation time 15-20 minutes
Cooking time 10-15 minutes
To serve 4

You will need

½ pint dark meat stock
dash Worcestershire sauce
2 tablespoons dry Madeira
4 slices ham, optional
4 pieces toast
4 fried eggs

Heat the meat stock in a saucepan and add the Worcestershire sauce and the Madeira. Simmer for 10 minutes. Arrange the ham on the pieces of freshly made toast and place the hot fried eggs on top. Pour the hot madeira sauce over the eggs and serve at once.

MIMOSA (EGG DUMPLINGS)

D. MIMOSER ÆGGEBOLLER
N. EGGEKULER

Savoury Egg Custard baked in flan case

These egg dumplings are often served in clear soups. They may also be used, replaced in the white of egg, to garnish a dish on the smörgåsbord.

Preparation time 8 minutes
Cooking time 10—12 minutes

You will need

3 hard-boiled eggs
raw egg yolk
salt
pepper

Shell the hard-boiled eggs and halve them lengthwise. Remove the yolks and pass these through a sieve. Add sufficient raw egg yolk to bind the mixture. Season with salt and pepper. Shape the egg-yolk mixture into small balls and place these as garnish in hot soup dishes. Alternatively, roll the egg-yolk balls in finely chopped parsley, put them back into the hard-boiled egg whites and serve as garnish for various dishes.

VARIATIONS
Chopped anchovies, anchovy paste, mayonnaise or liver pâté and truffles may be blended with the egg yolk before filling the whites. Serve these on the smörgåsbord.

55

FISH SOUFFLÉ

D. FISKEGRATIN
N. FISKESUFFLÉ
S. FISKESUFFLÉ

Preparation time 35 minutes
Cooking time 45—60 minutes
Oven temperature 400—425°F. Gas Mark 6—7
To serve 4

You will need

8 oz. fish fillets (cod or haddock)
2½ oz. butter
3½ oz. plain flour
scant ¾ pint (U.S. 1¾ cups) boiling milk
salt
pepper
juice of half lemon
chopped parsley
4 large eggs, separated
½ teaspoon baking powder

Cook the fish fillets for 5 minutes in salted, boiling water. Drain, remove the skin and flake the fish into small pieces. Melt the butter over low heat and stir in the flour; gradually add the boiling milk, stirring all the time, until all the milk has been absorbed. Cook for 2—3 minutes. Remove from the heat, season with salt and pepper to taste and leave to cool.
Add the lemon juice and chopped parsley. Stir in the egg yolks, one at a time, and add the cooked, flaked fish. Whisk the egg whites with the baking powder until stiff. Carefully fold the beaten egg whites into the fish mixture; pour into a well-greased soufflé dish and cook for 45 minutes to 1 hour in a hot oven. Serve the soufflé hot, immediately it is removed from the oven. This fish soufflé is delicious eaten with a melted butter or shrimp and asparagus sauce (see recipe page 69 and photograph page 50).

ASPARAGUS SOUFFLÉ

D. ASPARGESGRATIN
N. ASPARGESSUFFLÉ
S. SPARRISSUFFLÉ

Preparation time 30 minutes
Cooking time 45—60 minutes
Oven temperature 400—425°F. Gas Mark 6—7
To serve 4

You will need

1 lb. asparagus, fresh or canned
2½ oz. butter
3½ oz. plain flour
scant ¾ pint (U.S. 1¾ cups) boiling milk
salt
pepper
4 large eggs, separated
½ teaspoon baking powder

Clean the asparagus and cook in salted water for 10—12 minutes or until almost tender. (Drain canned asparagus and reserve the liquid). Drain the asparagus, but keep the water in which it was cooked, for the sauce.
Proceed to make soufflé mixture as in recipe above. Serve hot with Creamed Butter, Shrimp and Asparagus Sauce (see pages 66 and 69) or melted butter.

CAULIFLOWER SOUFFLÉ

D. BLOMKÅLSGRATIN
N. BLOMKÅLSUFFLÉ
S. BLOMKÅLSSUFFLÉ

Preparation time 30 minutes
Cooking time 45—60 minutes
Oven temperature 400—425°F. Gas Mark 6—7
To serve 4

You will need

1 cauliflower
2½ oz. butter
3½ oz. plain flour
scant ¾ pint (U.S. 1½ cups) boiling milk
salt
pepper
4 large egg yolks
4 large egg whites
½ teaspoon baking powder

Trim and rinse the cauliflower and cook it in boiling salt water for 5 minutes. Drain and cut into flowerets. Melt the butter over low heat and add the flour; stir and gradually add the boiling milk, stirring all the time, until all the milk has been absorbed. Cook for 2—3 minutes. Remove the saucepan from heat, season with salt and pepper and leave to cool.
Stir in the egg yolks, one at a time, and add the cooked cauliflower. Whisk the egg whites with the baking powder until stiff. Carefully fold in the egg whites, pour into a well-greased soufflé dish and cook for 45 minutes to 1 hour in a hot oven. Serve hot with Creamed Butter (see page 66), melted butter or tomato sauce.

Lemon Soup

Danish chervil soup and pancakes

STUFFED PANCAKES

S. FYLLDA PANNKAKOR

Preparation time   45 minutes
Cooking time   40 minutes
Oven temperature   475°F., Gas Mark 8
To serve   4-6

You will need

2 eggs
½ pint milk
2½ oz. plain flour
½ teaspoon salt
1 tablespoon melted butter
creamed shellfish (see page 77) *or*
creamed sweetbread (see page 94) *or*
creamed mushrooms (see page 110)
4 tablespoons grated Parmesan or Emmen-
    thaler cheese
2 tablespoons butter

Whisk the eggs with a little of the milk; add the flour and the salt, and continue to whisk to a smooth batter. Add the rest of the milk and finally stir in the melted butter. Do not have the batter too thick. Put only enough fat in the pan to cover the base when cooking the pancakes. Make thin pancakes. Put a couple of tablespoons of filling on each pancake and roll them up. Place the filled pancakes side by side, to fit closely in a greased fireproof dish. Sprinkle with grated cheese on top and dot with knobs of butter. Brown in a very hot oven for about 8 minutes until the cheese is melted.

VARIATION

The pancakes may be filled with chopped spinach or ham and covered with a Sauce Béchamel or Mornay before being sprinkled with cheese and cooked au gratin.

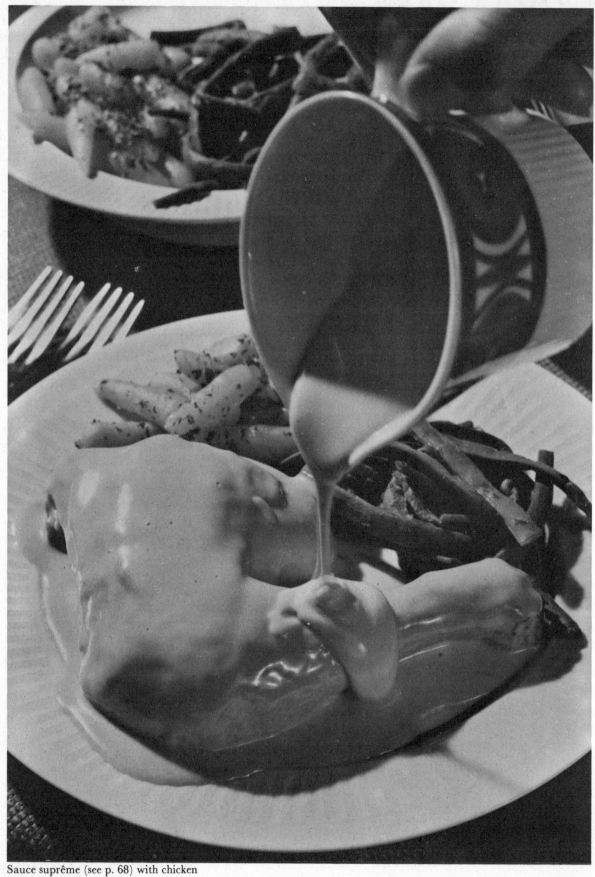

Sauce suprême (see p. 68) with chicken

SOUPS AND SAUCES

Soups do not form as important a part of Scandinavian cooking as they used to, or as they do in the Mediterranean countries, where they are on the menu every day. Nevertheless, there are plenty of excellent recipes for fish, meat, vegetable and sweet soups. The Norwegians have a delicious fish soup, made with sour cream, called 'Palesuppe', which is said to have originated in Bergen, and is certainly not to be missed by visitors to that city. The Danish fish soups are often made from the stock of poached fish, as in the case of Curry Soup. Meat soups tend to be thick and satisfying; they are often based on pork, as for example, Yellow Pea Soup, and are served in the winter as a main course followed only by pancakes or fruit and cheese. Mushroom, asparagus and cauliflower soups are all great favourites, as are clear chicken and beef soups which are served with flour and meat dumplings. The Danes are famous for two other soups: Chervil Soup, which has a highly distinctive flavour, and *Öllebröd*, literally beer-bread; this is one of the so-called sweet soups, and is made from Danish rye bread and a special sweetish dark beer with low alcoholic content. The sweet soups must surely be unique to Scandinavian cooking. Although out of favour today, some are worth mentioning: cold buttermilk, rosehip and lemon soups.

Sauces form an essential part of Scandinavian cooking—give a Scandinavian a meal without any gravy or sauce and he will be miserable. Plain, melted or brown butter is often served with meat or fish dishes and so are cold creamed butters. Other cold sauces include mayonnaise and variations of this. A word of warning about mayonnaise: it is a mistake to serve it with a hot dish! The French sauces Espagnole, béchamel and velouté are all used extensively and so are Hollandaise and Béarnaise sauces. Sauces with a very special Scandinavian character include those with such ingredients as horseradish and mustard, for example, those composed predominantly of cream, and game sauces enriched with cream and flavoured with redcurrant jelly or mushrooms.

CROÛTONS

D. BRØDTERNINGER

Preparation time 5 minutes
Cooking time 8 minutes
To serve 4

You will need

2 oz. butter
1½ oz. sugar
5 oz. white bread, trimmed and cut into
½-inch cubes

Melt the butter in a frying pan and toss the sugar and diced bread in it until the bread begins to turn golden brown. Remove the frying pan from the heat, but leave the croûtons to cool down in the pan as this will ensure that they remain crisp. Serve with sweet soups such as lemon, apple or cold buttermilk soup.

VARIATION

If croûtons are to be served with a savoury soup, omit the sugar.

CURRY SOUP

D. KARRYSUPPE
N. KARRISUPPE
S. CURRYSOPPA

The Norwegians and the Swedes use a meat stock as the base for this soup, but the Danes often use a fish stock.

Preparation time 15 minutes
Cooking time 10 minutes
To serve 4—6

You will need

2 oz. butter
1 small onion, sliced
1 clove of garlic, crushed
1 medium-sized cooking apple, peeled cored and finely grated
pinch thyme
½—1 teaspoon curry powder
2 oz. plain flour (optional)
3½ pints (U.S. 9 cups) fish stock
¼ pint (U.S. ⅔ cup) double cream

Melt the butter and gently sauté the sliced onion, garlic, apple and thyme. Stir in the curry powder and flour if used. Cook for 2—3 minutes; gradually add the fish stock and cook for a further 3—4 minutes. Just before serving, stir in the cream. Serve with hot French bread.

MUSHROOM SOUP

D. CHAMPIGNON SUPPE
N. SOPPSUPPE
S. SVAMPSOPPA

Preparation time 20 minutes
Cooking time 30 minutes
To serve 4

You will need

8 oz. mushrooms
½ pint (U.S. 1¼ cups) stock
1 oz. butter
salt and white pepper to taste
2—3 tablespoons plain flour
approximately 3 pints (U.S. approximately 7½ cups) stock
5 tablespoons double cream
1 teaspoon lemon juice
1—2 tablespoons Madeira or sherry (optional)

Slice the mushrooms and cook these in ½ pint of stock for about 10 minutes. Strain off the cooking liquid and keep this. In another saucepan melt the butter and add the mushrooms; fry for a few minutes, season with salt and pepper and sprinkle the flour over them. Gradually add the hot cooking liquid and the remainder of the stock. Boil the soup for 3—5 minutes. Add the cream and lemon juice and stir in the wine. Taste for seasoning and serve hot with hot French bread (see photograph page 63).

DANISH CHERVIL SOUP

D. KØRVELSUPPE

This soup has a delightful and distinctive flavour and is, in addition, very decorative with its colour scheme of pale green and yellow.

Preparation time 25 minutes
Cooking time 25 minutes
To serve 4

You will need

3 pints (U.S. 7½ cups) hot stock (preferably pork or ham)
2 large carrots, sliced
3 oz. butter
3 tablespoons plain flour
salt to taste
pepper to taste
3 level tablespoons fresh chervil, minced or chopped
2 smiling eggs, halved (see page 52)

Pour the stock into a saucepan and bring to the boil with the sliced carrots; cook until carrots are tender, then strain and reserve the liquid. Melt the butter in another saucepan, add the flour and cook over a low heat until the mixture is smooth. Gradually stir in the hot stock, whilst continuing to cook over low heat. Season with salt and pepper and boil gently for 3—5 minutes. Add the cooked carrots and heat these before finally adding the minced chervil. Remove the saucepan from the heat at once, as the chervil will lose its delicate flavour and fresh, green colour if it is allowed to boil in the soup. Place half a Smiling Egg in each soup plate and carefully ladle the hot soup over each (see photograph page 58).

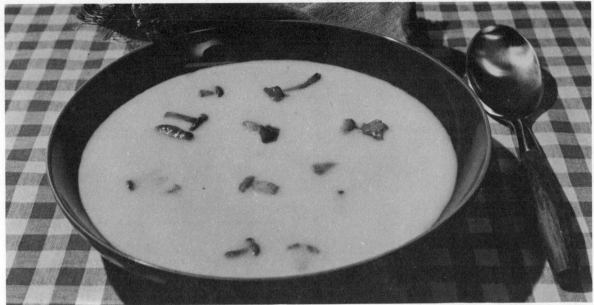

Mushroom soup

YELLOW PEA SOUP WITH PORK 1.

D. GULE ÆRTER OG FLÆSK

This is perhaps the most popular winter soup in Scandinavia. The meat stock can be made from either slightly salted pork or ham, but is also delicious if it comes from cooking Salt Goose, Salt Duck or Rolled Veal Sausage (see pages 102 and 31). The Danish version differs slightly from those of Norway and Sweden. In Sweden Yellow Pea Soup is said to be on the menu in many restaurants every Thursday during the winter season, traditionally followed by pancakes and jam. In Denmark *Æbleskiver* or pancakes may be served after the soup (see photograph page 58).

Preparation time 40 minutes
Cooking time 2½ hours
To serve 4—6

You will need

12 oz. dried yellow peas
2 pints (U.S. 5 cups) boiled, cold water
2—3 lb. slightly salted belly of pork (in one piece)
2—3 pints (U.S. 5—7½ cups) water
bouquet garni
2 leeks
8 shallots
8 oz. potatoes
½ celeriac, peeled
3—4 carrots
fresh or dried thyme to taste

Rinse the peas and soak them overnight in some of the boiled water. Bring the peas quickly to the boil in the same water in which they were soaked. Skim the soup very well and leave it to simmer, covered with a lid for 1—2 hours, until the peas are tender; rub them through a sieve. Meanwhile, place the piece of pork in another saucepan with the remainder of water (if very salty, soak for a couple of hours first). Bring the pork to the boil and skim very well. Cut the green tops off the leeks and tie them up with the bouquet garni. Add to the meat and cook for 1—1¼ hours until almost tender. Add the onions, potatoes, celeriac, carrots and the remainder of the leeks and cook until tender. Remove the vegetables, slice the onions and leeks and dice the other vegetables. When tender remove the pork from the soup and keep it warm. Discard the bouquet garni, skim the fat off the soup and stir the pea purée into the soup. It should have a thick, creamy consistency. Remove the stalks from the thyme and crumble the leaves between the fingers; add to the soup. Replace the vegetables and heat the soup thoroughly without boiling.

Traditionally, a bowl of soup is eaten side by side with the sliced pork, and with a thick, boiled, spicy sausage—rather like a Cumberland sausage. These should be accompanied by strong French mustard, pickled beetroot (see page 32) and dark rye bread. Ice-cold snaps and lager make this dish still more enjoyable by creating a nice glowing feeling, which is often badly needed on a cold winter's evening in Scandinavia.

Note

If yellow peas are cooked in a pressure cooker, allow 10—15 minutes at 15 lb. pressure. They need not then be rubbed through a sieve.

YELLOW PEA SOUP WITH PORK 2.

N. GUL ERTESUPPE MED FLESK
S. ÄRTER OCH FLÄSK

Preparation time 25 minutes
Cooking time 2½ hours
To serve 4

You will need

12 oz. dried yellow peas
4 pints (U.S. 10 cups) water
1½ lb. lightly-salted side of pork
   (in one piece)
1 onion, quartered
1 teaspoon chopped marjoram, thyme *or*
   ½ teaspoon ground ginger
salt (optional)

Rinse the peas and soak them overnight in the water. Cook in the same water and remove any shells that float on to the surface. Skim the soup well and add the pork, onion and herbs or ginger. Cover the saucepan with a lid and simmer the soup until the peas and pork are tender (1—2 hours, depending on the type of yellow peas used). Remove the pork, cut it into slices and serve it separately with mustard. Season the soup with salt if necessary, but be careful as the salted pork may already have seasoned the soup sufficiently.

LEMON SOUP

D. CITRONSUPPE

The Greeks have a marvellous savoury lemon soup but this Danish lemon soup is sweet, and is a great favourite with children.

Preparation time 30 minutes
Cooking time 20 minutes
To serve 4—6

You will need

1 oz. butter
1½ oz. plain flour
3 pints (U.S. 7½ cups) water
thinly pared rind and juice of 2 large lemons
2 egg yolks
2—2½ oz. sugar

Melt the butter in a saucepan over low heat and add the flour. When this is absorbed, add the water gradually so that the mixture does not become lumpy. Add the lemon rind and boil for about 10 minutes. Meanwhile, whisk the egg yolks with the sugar until they are frothy and white; add the lemon juice and whisk again. Remove the saucepan from the heat and strain the sauce on to the egg mixture. Return to the saucepan and heat carefully. Take care not to let the soup boil after the addition of the egg yolks or it will curdle. Serve with either whipped cream, small rusks or croûtons (see recipe page 61 and photograph page 57).

ROSEHIP SOUP

D. HYBENSUPPE
N. NYPESUPPE
S. NYPONSOPPA

This is a sweet soup which may be served in the Scandinavian manner before the main course to take the edge off your appetite.

Preparation time 20—30 minutes
Cooking time 30—45 minutes
To serve 4—6

You will need

1 lb. fresh rosehips *or*
   4 oz. dried rosehips
2 pints (U.S. 5 cups) water
peel of 1 lemon
2—3 oz. sugar
1½—2 tablespoons cornflour *or* potato
   flour, dissolved in a little cold water
1 teaspoon lemon juice
½ oz. blanched shredded almonds
whipped double cream

Wash the fresh rosehips or soak the dried ones for 48 hours in 2 pints of water. Boil them in the water with the lemon peel, over gentle heat, for about 20 minutes. Rub through a sieve and pour into a saucepan, add the sugar and bring to the boil. Add the cornflour and gently boil the soup for 2—3 minutes. Draw the saucepan away from the heat and add the lemon juice. Serve the soup hot or cold. Sprinkle with shredded almonds and serve chilled whipped cream with it.
The colour of this soup is delightful when made with fresh rosehips.

Chilled Buttermilk Soup

CHILLED BUTTERMILK SOUP

D. KÆRNEMÆLKSKOLDSKÅL
N. KJERNEMELKSKALDSKÅL

This refreshing chilled, sweet soup can be served either before or after the main course. I have known people who profess to not liking buttermilk, eating it with great relish! It tastes particularly good on a hot summer evening. Serve it with small macaroons or rusks.

Preparation time 10 minutes
To serve   6

You will need

2 egg yolks
3—4 oz. sugar
juice and grated rind of 1 lemon
3 pints (U.S. 7½ cups) buttermilk
¼ pint double cream, whipped
1 vanilla pod *or*
   vanilla sugar to taste

Beat the egg yolks together with the sugar, lemon juice and grated lemon rind. Cut the vanilla pod in half, scrape the seeds into the egg mixture, and stir in the buttermilk or add the vanilla sugar to taste. Chill thoroughly, preferably in a refrigerator, and serve with chilled whipped cream.

FLOUR DUMPLINGS

D. MELBOLLER
N. MELBOLLER
S. KLIMP

These are usually served in clear meat soups, but also in sweet soups. In Norway a little ground cardamom is often added as seasoning; in Sweden, either cardamom or 2—3 grated blanched almonds are added.

Preparation time 30 minutes
Cooking time   5—10 minutes

You will need

4½ oz. butter
4½ oz. plain flour
scant ½ pint (U.S. 1 cup) water
4—5 eggs
salt
pinch sugar (optional)

Melt the butter in a saucepan and add the flour. Cook for 2—3 minutes, but do not let it brown. Gradually add the water, stirring all the time, until the mixture is smooth. Remove the saucepan from the heat. Beat the eggs and add them one at a time to the hot mixture, beating vigorously as you do so. The number of eggs to be used depends on their size; the mixture should be thick enough to be of dropping consistency. Finally, add the salt. Shape the dough with two teaspoons and place the flour dumplings in boiling, salted water. Simmer for 5—10 minutes according to their size. Lift them out with a slotted spoon and leave until ready to serve. Gently heat the dumplings in the soup, but be careful not to let the soup boil, or the dumplings will disintegrate.

VARIATIONS

The flour dumplings may be shaped by pressing the dough through a forcing bag and cutting it off into 1-inch pieces, with a knife dipped in boiling water. The dumplings may be placed in boiling water to which cold water is added, as soon as it reaches boiling point. Repeat this 3 times by which time the dumplings will be cooked.
Note
The dumplings may be made one day in advance. As soon as they are cooked immerse them in cold water. Transfer them to a plate and cover with a clean, white cloth. Leave in a cool place until the following day when they should be heated gently in the soup.

MEAT DUMPLINGS

D. KØDBOLLER
N. KJÖTTBOLLER
S. FRIKADELLER

These meat dumplings are generally served together with the flour dumplings in clear meat soups.

Preparation time 30 minutes
Cooking time   4—5 minutes

You will need

farce (recipe 1 or 2, see pages 90 and 92)
water
salt

Shape the farce with two teaspoons and place the small meat dumplings carefully in salted boiling water. Simmer for 4—5 minutes until cooked. Lift out the dumplings with a slotted spoon and when ready to serve, heat them gently in the soup.

BRAIN BALLS

D. HJERNEBOLLER

Preparation time 30 minutes
Cooking time   5 minutes
To serve   2—3

You will need

1 calf's brain (approximately 8 oz.)
white breadcrumbs
1 egg
lemon juice
crushed garlic
salt
pepper
chopped parsley
fat for deep frying (optional)

Place the calf's brain in cold water for a couple of hours and then scald it with boiling water; cool and remove the outer membrane. Weigh the brain and put it through a mincer three times with half its weight in breadcrumbs. Add the egg, a few drops of lemon juice, a little garlic, salt and pepper and the chopped parsley. Stir the mixture thoroughly to combine all the ingredients. Shape into balls and cook in deep hot fat for 2—3 minutes, or drop into barely simmering water until the balls rise to the surface. Drain and serve hot.

CREAMED BUTTER

D. RØRT SMØR

This 'butter sauce' is so delicious that I have known English friends exclaim with surprise when told how easy it is to make. It could hardly be simpler, as you will see from the recipe below. The whole secret is to cream the butter enough. Creamed butter is served with freshly boiled vegetables.

Preparation time 15—20 minutes
To serve   4—6

You will need

7—8 oz. butter
a few drops of warm water

Place the butter in a fairly large bowl which has been slightly warmed. Cream the butter until it is white—this will take a good 10—15 minutes unless, of course, you have an electric mixer, which will do the job for you in less than half the time. Add a few drops of warm water to speed the creaming. Serve with vegetables (see photograph page 86).

VARIATIONS
1. Add some chopped parsley just before serving.
2. If served with fish, add a few drops of lemon juice and a little pepper.

TARTARE BUTTER

D. TARTARSMØR

Preparation time 30 minutes
To serve   4—6

You will need

7—8 oz. butter
1 teaspoon Worcestershire sauce
1 teaspoon French mustard
1 teaspoon lemon juice
1 teaspoon chopped parsley

Cream the butter as in the recipe for Creamed Butter (see above). Add the Worcestershire sauce, mustard, lemon juice and parsley and stir well. Serve with cold egg dishes; as a spread for open sandwiches or canapés; or with fried fish, steak or chops.

HORSERADISH BUTTER

D. PEBERRODSSMØR

Preparation time 25 minutes
To serve 4—6

You will need

7—8 oz. butter
1 oz. freshly grated horseradish

Cream the butter as in the recipe for Creamed Butter (see page 66). Add the grated horseradish and serve with roast beef, boiled or fried fish or serve as a spread for open sandwiches or canapés.

ANCHOVY BUTTER

D. ANSJOSSMØR

Preparation time 20 minutes
To serve 4—6

You will need

7—8 oz. butter
½ oz. anchovies

Cream the butter as in the recipe for Creamed Butter (see page 66). Chop the anchovies very finely and add to the butter. Serve with steaks, chops and grilled or fried fish or serve as a spread for open sandwiches or canapés.

DILL BUTTER

D. DILDSMØR

Preparation time 30 minutes
To serve 4—6

You will need

7—8 oz. butter
3 hard-boiled egg yolks, very finely chopped
2—3 tablespoons chopped dill
ground black pepper to taste

Cream the butter as in the recipe for Creamed Butter (see page 66). Add the chopped egg yolks and dill and season with pepper. Serve with smoked salmon, grilled fish or as a spread for open sandwiches or canapés.

SHELLFISH BUTTER

D. SKALDDYRSSMÖR
N. SKALLDYRSMÖR
S. SKALDJÜRSSMÖR

Lobster, crayfish or prawns may be used for this recipe.

Preparation time 20 minutes
Cooking time 15 minutes

You will need

shells of 1—2 boiled lobsters *or*
    shells of about 20 boiled crayfish *or*
    shells of 8—12 oz. prawns
1½ oz. butter
water

Pound the shells in a mortar, then add the butter. Work the mixture with a pestle until smooth. Put the mixture into a saucepan and fry carefully over gentle heat; do not let it brown. Add just sufficient water to cover the shells. Bring the mixture to the boil. Strain off the shells and discard them. Leave the liquid to cool. When completely cold, remove the butter on top and use it at once. The liquid may be used in sauces, stews or soups, but should not be stored. The shellfish butter may be used in sauces, fillings and soups, prepared from fish or shellfish, to give flavour and colour to the dish. It should not be kept unless it can be deep frozen. In this case melt it and let it boil until it looks clear; cool, and when the butter solidifies, roll it into balls and deep freeze it.

VINAIGRETTE

Preparation time 5 minutes

You will need

6 tablespoons olive oil
2 tablespoons tarragon or wine vinegar
salt to taste
pinch black pepper

Mix the ingredients by shaking or whisking them together. Taste for seasoning. Vinaigrette is used with green salads, salads of raw or cooked vegetables, fish, shellfish or meat.

VARIATION

Herb dressing: Add 1—2 teaspoons chopped herbs, such as dill, chives, chervil or tarragon, to the recipe above. Mix the ingredients and taste for seasoning.

TOMATO DRESSING

S. TOMATDRESSING

Preparation time 5 minutes

You will need

vinaigrette dressing (see page 67)
1—2 tablespoons tomato purée
½ teaspoon grated onion (optional)

Mix the ingredients and taste for seasoning. Use
with vegetable and fish salads.

ONION DRESSING

S. LÖKDRESSING

Preparation time 5 minutes

You will need

vinaigrette (see page 67)
1 teaspoon grated onion *or*
    1 pinch onion salt

Mix the ingredients and taste for seasoning. Use
with vegetable, fish and meat salads.

BASIC LIGHT SAUCE
(SAUCE VELOUTÉ)

The liquid for this sauce usually consists of either
fish, meat, poultry or vegetable stock, but sometimes a stock may be made from a carcass or bones.
Commercially prepared bouillon cubes may also
be used, but always taste the stock before using it
to check that it is not too salty. Sometimes a light
sauce is thickened twice: first with butter and flour
and then with egg yolk and cream which is added
after the liquid. The yolk is stirred with the cream
in a sauceboat and the hot sauce is then whisked
into the egg mixture. Alternatively, the egg thickening may be whisked into the sauce, but be careful
not to let the sauce boil, or the yolk may curdle.
Various flavours, such as parsley, dill, chives, lemon,
horseradish, mushrooms, asparagus, mustard, capers
or shellfish may be added to the basic light sauce.
A sauce suprême is basic light sauce to which thick
cream and a little butter is added.

Preparation time 5 minutes
Cooking time   10 minutes
To serve   4

You will need

1¼ oz. butter
1 oz. plain flour
½—¾ pint (U.S. 1¼—1¾ cups) boiling stock
salt and white pepper to taste

Melt the butter in a heavy saucepan over low heat;
add the flour and stir. Cook the roux gently without
browning it for 2—3 minutes. Remove from heat
and add the liquid all at once, whisking vigorously
until blended. Bring to the boil while stirring, and
simmer over low heat for at least 5 minutes. Season
and use as required.

HORSERADISH SAUCE

D. PEBERRODSSAUCE
N. PEPPERROTSAUS
S. PEPPARROTSSÅS

If the horseradish is grated in advance, cover it up
or it will change its colour to an ugly blue-grey.

Preparation time 10 minutes
Cooking time   12 minutes
To serve   4

You will need

basic light sauce (see opposite)
2—3 tablespoons finely grated horseradish
2—3 tablespoons double cream *or*
    ½ oz. butter

Boil the basic light sauce and reduce it to about ½ pint
(U.S. 1¼ cups). Add the grated horseradish and taste
for seasoning. Do not let the horseradish boil or the
gravy may taste bitter. Remove from the heat and
stir in the cream or the cold butter. Serve the horseradish sauce hot with poached fish (such as pike),
beef, or salt goose or duck (see page 102).

COLD HORSERADISH
CREAM SAUCE

D. KOLD FLØDEPEBERRODS-
SAUCE
N. PEPPERROTFLØTE
S. PEPPARROTSGRÄDDE

Take care to cover the freshly grated horseradish
until ready for use, or it will become discoloured.

Preparation time 5 minutes
To serve 4—6

You will need

1 oz. grated horseradish
½ pint double cream, whipped

Add the freshly grated horseradish to the cream and stir gently. Serve this refreshing and simple cold sauce with pickled duck or goose; boiled or roast beef; chicken or fish.

VARIATION
Freeze the horseradish cream sauce in small containers and just before serving, remove from containers and arrange on lettuce leaves or in hollowed-out tomatoes.

MUSTARD SAUCE

D. SENNEPSSAUCE
N. SENNEPSAUS
S. SENEPSSÅS

Preparation time 10 minutes
Cooking time 8 minutes
To serve 4

You will need

½ oz. butter
2 tablespoons plain flour
approximately ¾ pint (U.S. approximately 1¾ cups) creamy milk
salt
pinch pepper or paprika
1—2 tablespoons prepared mustard *or* mustard seeds

Melt the butter and add the flour. Cook for 1—2 minutes without browning; gradually add the milk whilst stirring. Bring to the boil over gentle heat, stirring all the time. Taste for seasoning. Add the mustard or the whole mustard seeds, which should be crushed in a little water. Serve with boiled fish such as cod or *lutfisk* or grilled herring and mackerel.

PICKLED SALMON SAUCE

S. GRAVLAXSÅS

Preparation time 10 minutes
To serve 4

You will need

2 tablespoons mustard
1 tablespoon sugar
1 egg yolk
2 tablespoons vinegar
7 tablespoons oil
chopped dill
salt
ground white pepper

Mix the mustard, sugar, egg yolk and vinegar. Pour the oil into the mixture, stirring thoroughly. Add plenty of dill and season with salt and pepper. Serve with pickled salmon or other pickled fish, boiled lobster or crab.

SHRIMP SAUCE

D. REJE SAUCE

If possible use the shellfish butter on page 67 for making the basic light sauce for this recipe.

Preparation time 15 minutes
Cooking time 12 minutes
To serve 4

You will need

basic light sauce (page 68)
4½ oz. cooked, peeled prawns or shrimps
1 egg yolk

Boil the basic light sauce and reduce to ½ pint. Add the prawns and heat gently. Stir the egg yolk with a little of the hot sauce in a cup and add this to the remainder in the saucepan. Remove from heat and serve at once with fish dumplings, Norwegian fish mousse, or fish soufflé (see pages 77 and 56).
Note
4 oz. cooked asparagus may be added to the sauce.

Filleting mackerel

Preparing pickled mackerel

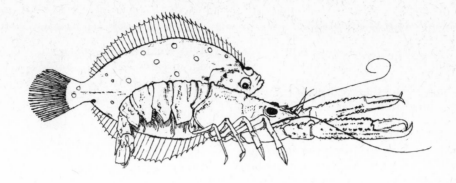

FISH

Nowhere is fish better than in Norway. Poached halibut served with a thick yellow Hollandaise sauce and whole poached cod with plain, melted butter are both delicacies of the highest order. The reason for this is simple—the fish is fresh. Fish killed and cooked within hours of catching can never fail to be delicious. Visitors to the fishmarkets in Bergen or in Copenhagen will be familiar with the sight of fish being kept alive in fish tanks until bought for consumption. Why, oh why, must we who live in this island put up with the delays in delivery and thus suffer the inevitable stale fish? If you start with fresh fish, it follows logically that the preparation and cooking should be simple, so as not to drown its subtle flavour. Hence the relative simplicity of Scandinavian fish dishes compared with those of the French, whose delicious sauces often disguise the rather poorer quality of the fish. As a rule, fish is poached in a court bouillon which contains vinegar instead of wine. Alternatively, the fish is stuffed with parsley or other herbs and fried in butter. The mackerel, the herring and the garfish, with its green bones, are all cooked in this way. Unfortunately, outside Scandinavia one rarely sees the garfish on the fishmonger's slab.

The Baltic Sea yields a particularly delicious small herring, called *strømming* in Swedish. The Swedes are very imaginative when it comes to dealing with this, whether fresh or salted. Danish plaice are large, thick and fully as delicious as that aristocrat of flat fish, the sole. Both are often accompanied by creamy sauces in which the Danes make free use of asparagus, mushrooms and shellfish.

The smoking or curing of fish has been practised for a long time in Scandinavia, first in the home and later on an industrial scale, not only for the home market, but also for export. Herring, mackerel and cod are often smoked, as well as salmon and eel. Many English people find the idea of eating eel rather alarming; this is easy to understand as English eels are rather large and forbidding, whereas the Scandinavian ones, like the Dutch, are small, slender and quite delicious. Cured salmon or *gravlaks* and lime-cured codfish, known as *lutfisk*—a traditional Christmas dish in Norway and Sweden—are two more Scandinavian specialities. Sweden is also renowned for its crayfish, Denmark for the oysters from the Limfjord, and Norway for its superb lobsters and prawns. Finally, Norway has a magnificent dish, fish soufflé—a fish farce, which is the Scandinavian equivalent of the French *quenelle*.

POACHED HERRINGS

D. KOGT SILD

Herrings are among the cheapest fish. They are also very rich and should therefore always be poached in the following way:

Place the cleaned herrings in a saucepan with water and vinegar (3 parts water to 1 part vinegar), salt, whole peppercorns and a small onion. Bring the herrings to the boil, skim well and simmer over gentle heat for 5—6 minutes. Serve with new boiled potatoes and ice-cold butter and possibly a white wine vinegar.

BRAISED HERRINGS

D. OVNSTEGTE SILD

Clean and fillet the herrings and place them in a buttered ovenproof dish in layers, with skinned chopped tomatoes, finely chopped mushrooms, shallots, and a little garlic. Fill up the dish, dot with butter, sprinkle with salt and freshly ground pepper, and braise the herrings in a moderate oven for about 15 minutes. Serve with warm French bread and a green salad.

FRIED FRESH HERRINGS

D. STEGT SILD
N. STEKT SILD
S. STEKT FÄRSK SILL ELLER STRÖMMING

Preparation time 20 minutes
Cooking time 7—8 minutes
To serve 4

You will need

2 lb. herrings
2—3 teaspoons salt
3—4 tablespoons coarse rye flour, oatmeal or browned breadcrumbs
butter
dill, chives or parsley (optional)

Clean the fish and, if you like, remove the backbone. Wash the fish thoroughly and allow to drain. Add salt and toss in flour, oatmeal or browned breadcrumbs. Fry until golden brown on both sides. Sprinkle with dill, chives or parsley and serve with boiled or creamed potatoes and a green salad.
Note
These fried herrings may be used in the recipe for soused herrings (see page 18).

HERRING À LA OPRIS

S. STRÖMMING À LA OPRIS

This is a speciality of the restaurant 'The Opera Cellar' in Stockholm.

Preparation time 30 minutes
Cooking time 7—8 minutes
To serve 4

You will need

2 lb. small fresh herrings
2 egg yolks
generous ¼ pint (U.S. ⅔ cup) double cream
3—4 tablespoons coarse rye flour *or* oatmeal
2—3 teaspoons salt
butter

Clean the herrings and remove the backbones. Wash thoroughly and drain. Stir the egg yolks into the cream and soak the fish in this mixture for at least 1 hour. Lift out the herrings carefully, having folded them in two so that the cream mixture does not drip off. Toss quickly in coarse rye flour or oatmeal and salt and fry immediately until crisp and brown on both sides. Serve the fish hot or cold with boiled potatoes

---

MACHINE COD

D. MASKINTORSK

The extraordinary name for this Danish dish is due to the fact that it used to be made in a container with a tightly fitting lid called 'the machine'. A fireproof casserole with a tight-fitting lid can obviously be used with equally good results.

Preparation time 20—25 minutes
Cooking time 25—30 minutes
Oven temperature 375°F. Gas Mark 5
To serve 4

You will need

1½ lb. cod fillets
salt
1—2 teaspoons curry powder
1—2 tablespoons plain flour
2 medium-sized onions, finely chopped
½ piece celeriac, scraped and grated
2 oz. butter
scant ¼ pint (U.S. ½ cup) white wine
scant ¼ pint (U.S. ½ cup) cream

Cut the cod fillets into 2-inch pieces and season with salt and curry powder. Put the chopped onions and half of the prepared celeriac into the base of a well-greased fireproof casserole. Dip the fish in the flour and place on top of the vegetables. Spread the other half of the celeriac on top of the cod; season with a little salt and put knobs of butter on top. Pour over the white wine and the cream. Cook for about 20—30 minutes in a fairly hot oven. Serve French bread with this dish.

POACHED COD

D. KOGT TORSK
N. KOKT TORSK
S. KOKT TORSK

Poached cod need not be frowned upon. It can be a delightful dish if it is served with many savoury accompaniments—provided, of course, that the fish is really fresh.

Preparation time 30 minutes
Cooking time 12—15 minutes
To serve 4

You will need

1 medium-sized cod, weighing 3—4 lb.
salt
water, to each 2 pints (U.S. 5 cups) add
 1½ oz. salt and 4 tablespoons wine vinegar
3—4 whole peppercorns
2 bay leaves

Clean the cod and rinse it several times under running cold water. Cut the cod into 1½-inch steaks and sprinkle these with salt. Leave to stand for 15 minutes or more. Rinse the fish in cold water again. Add salt and vinegar to water in a saucepan, with peppercorns and bay leaves, and bring to the boil. Place the cod steaks in the boiling water, cover the saucepan with a tightly fitting lid and bring the water gently to the boil again. Remove the saucepan from heat and leave to stand, still covered with the lid, for about 10 minutes. Drain and place the fish on a hot serving dish, covered with a napkin to absorb any excess moisture. Serve at once with either hot melted butter or mustard sauce (see page 69) and small boiled potatoes. As accompaniments serve *all* or *any* of the following: chopped hard-boiled egg (egg white and yolk chopped separately), chopped parsley, grated horseradish, capers, chopped pickled beetroot (see recipe page 32 and photograph page 76).
Note
Any left-over cod can be used for Fish Salad (see page 24). The fish stock may be used for the Curry Soup (see page 62) if less salt is used for the court-bouillon.

CRAYFISH

S. KRÄFTOR

Crayfish are a great delicacy in Scandinavia, particularly in Sweden, where the season is open from 7th August till 1st November. Catching them with nets is a popular nocturnal sport during the early part of the season. Crayfish parties are often given outside during the late summer evenings, lit with paper lanterns hung in the trees—and by the August moon.

It is very important that crayfish should be alive when put into boiling water. Wash the live crayfish thoroughly in cold water; boil water, salt and dill for 2—3 minutes, remove the dill, and then plunge the crayfish into the water (30 crayfish to 6 pints of water, 5 tablespoons salt and pickling dill). Cover and cook for 6—7 minutes. Add more dill, cool in the liquor and keep in the refrigerator before serving. Arrange on a serving dish. Garnish with more heads of dill. Serve with toast and butter.

COD'S ROE

D. TORSKEROGN
N. TORSKEROGN
S. TORSKROM

Preparation time 20—25 minutes
Cooking time 30 minutes
To serve 4

You will need

1½ lb. cod's roes
water
salt
1 beaten egg
brown breadcrumbs
salt
pepper
2—3 oz. butter

Wrap the cod roes carefully in greaseproof paper and cook in boiling salted water for about 20 minutes or more, according to their sizes. Remove from the saucepan and leave to cool on a plate, with another plate on top to weight them down slightly. Remove the greaseproof paper and cut the roes into 2-inch slices. Dip these in beaten egg and breadcrumbs seasoned with salt and pepper. Fry the roe in butter over medium heat for a couple of minutes on each side, until cooked and golden brown. Serve with boiled potatoes and tartare sauce (see page 26).

VARIATIONS

1. As an alternative, dip the sliced cod's roe in seasoned flour only before frying.
2. Arrange the fried roes on a serving dish and garnish each slice with a wedge of lemon, a fillet of anchovy, a few capers and some freshly grated horseradish.

PICKLED SALMON

D. GRAVLAKS
N. GRAVLAKS
S. GRAVAD LAX

This is an ancient Swedish recipe which has for a long time also been popular in Norway and more recently in Denmark. The dish is best made in the spring, particularly as this is a time of year when you can get fresh supplies of dill. The Norwegians actually use pine twigs as well as dill. The saltpetre is used to retain the delicate red colour of the fish. Connoisseurs will tell you that they prefer this dish to smoked salmon. It is not, of course, a cheap dish but it is certainly worth trying for a grand occasion, particularly as it is really very simple to prepare.

Preparation time 25 minutes
To serve   10—12

You will need

4½ lb. middle-cut salmon (in one piece)
2 tablespoons coarse salt
1 teaspoon crushed white peppercorns
2 tablespoons sugar
pinch saltpetre
dill

Clean the fish and remove the bones so that you have two big fillets. Do not rinse the fish in water, but scrape and dry it with a cloth. Place a large quantity of dill in a large dish. Mix the salt, pepper, sugar and saltpetre and rub this mixture into the flesh of the salmon fillets. Sprinkle them with sprigs of dill and place one fillet (skin side down) on top of the dill in the dish. Place the second fillet (skin side up) on top of this, in such a way that the thick end of one fillet is under the thin end of the other. Scatter more dill on top (as you will see, you can hardly use too much dill) and place a heavy plate or board on top of the fish. Keep in a cold place—not a refrigerator—for 16—24 hours. Scrape all the spices off the salmon and cut into thin slices; arrange these either flat or rolled up on a serving dish and scatter with more fresh dill. Serve with mustard sauce (see page 69).

VARIATION
Cut salmon into thick slices, garnish these with lemon wedges and serve with either creamed spinach or poached eggs. The skin of the pickled salmon can be cut into small pieces, grilled and served in the same way.

PICKLED TROUT OR MACKEREL

Trout and mackerel can be pickled in the same way as salmon. For each pound of fish, use 1 teaspoon coarse salt, ¼ teaspoon crushed white peppercorns, 1 teaspoon sugar, pinch saltpetre and plenty of dill. One small glass of brandy may be poured over the fish. This is not entirely necessary, though there is no doubt that it improves the flavour (see photograph page 70).

FISH FARCE

D. FISKEFARS
N. FISKFARS
S. FISKFÄRS

Preparation time 30—40 minutes
Cooking time   10 minutes

You will need

1 lb. fish fillets
2 teaspoons salt
pinch white pepper
5 tablespoons plain flour *or*
   potato flour
2 oz. butter
2 eggs
1—1½ pints (U.S. 2½—3¾ cups) single cream
   or top of milk

Rinse the fillets and dry them thoroughly. Skin and mince them 2—3 times and mix with the seasoning and flour. Stir the farce vigorously and work in the softened butter. Add the eggs one at a time and gradually add the liquid. If the farce curdles, stand the bowl in hot water and whisk briskly until smooth again. Check the seasoning. Shape the farce into small round balls with the aid of two spoons dipped into hot water. Bring approximately 2 pints of salted water or stock to the boil then cook one ball to test the consistency. Add more egg if the farce is too soft, or milk if it is too stiff. Serve in shrimp and asparagus sauce, basic light sauce or with mock turtle (see pages 69, 68 and 84).

VARIATION
The farce may be cooked in a ring-shaped mould in the same way as Norwegian Fish Mousse. Serve it with Shrimp and Asparagus Sauce (see recipes pages 77 and 69 and photograph opposite).

Fish mould

Poached Cod

CREAMED SHELLFISH

D. SKALDDYRSSTUVNING
N. SKALLDYRSSTUING
S. SKALDJURSSTUVNINGAR

Creamed shellfish made from fresh lobster, prawns or crab have a stronger colour and flavour when the butter used in the sauce is completely, or partly, replaced by shellfish butter. The shell juices may also be used in the preparation of the sauce.

Preparation time 20 minutes
Cooking time 5 minutes
To serve 4—6

You will need

1—2 boiled lobsters *or*
  8 oz. can lobster *or*
  12 oz. fresh prawns *or*
  1—2 oz. cans prawns *or*
  1—2 boiled crabs *or*
  10 oz. can crab meat
2—3 tablespoons shellfish butter
  (see page 67)
2 tablespoons flour
$\frac{1}{2}$ pint (U.S. $1\frac{1}{4}$ cups) shellfish liquid or
  fish stock
$\frac{1}{4}$ pint (U.S. $\frac{2}{3}$ cup) double cream
$\frac{1}{2}$—1 tablespoon brandy
pinch pepper
pinch cayenne pepper
pinch ground cloves

Remove the meat from the fresh shellfish, or drain canned shellfish, and cut the meat of larger shellfish into pieces. Melt the shellfish butter in a saucepan and add the flour. Cook over gentle heat for 1—2 minutes without browning. Gradually stir in the shellfish liquid until smooth and stir in the double cream. Continue to cook over gentle heat for 3—5 minutes. Add the brandy and season with pepper, cayenne and ground cloves. Place the shellfish in the sauce and heat gently without boiling, as this makes the shellfish tough. Serve hot as a filling for omelettes or pastry shells (see page 144) or serve with boiled rice.

NORWEGIAN FISH MOUSSE

N. FISKEPUDDING

This light and airy fish pudding is undoubtedly one of the highlights of the Norwegian cuisine.

Preparation time 30 minutes
Cooking time 1 hour
Oven temperature 400°F. Gas Mark 6
To serve 4—6

You will need

$2\frac{3}{4}$ lb. whole fish (pike, haddock or cod) *or*
  1 lb. fresh fillets
2 teaspoons salt
pinch white pepper
$1\frac{1}{2}$ tablespoons potato flour
$\frac{1}{2}$ pint (U.S. $1\frac{1}{4}$ cups) creamy milk
generous $\frac{1}{4}$ pint (U.S. $\frac{2}{3}$ cup) single or double
  cream

Clean the whole fish, fillet and skin it, or rinse the fillets and dry them thoroughly. Skin the fillets and mince these 2—3 times and mix with the seasonings and potato flour (mince them a further 2—3 times, if you want the mousse to be really finely textured). Stir the farce vigorously and gradually incorporate the milk and cream, beating all the time. Butter a $2\frac{1}{2}$—3 pint oblong mould and coat it with breadcrumbs. Add the mixture until the mould is three-quarters full. Cover with buttered waxed paper or aluminium foil and cook in a water-bath either on top of the stove or in a fairly hot oven for about 1 hour. Invert the mould very carefully and garnish the fish pudding with parsley, lemon, shrimps or lobster. Serve with Hollandaise or mustard sauce, shellfish butter or shrimp sauce (see pages 69 and 67). The fish farce may be flavoured with a pinch of nutmeg or with 1—2 small anchovy fillets, which should be minced together with the fish.

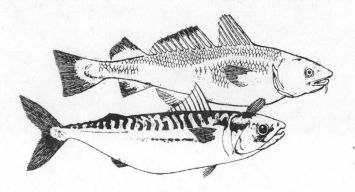

Glazed gammon, Danish cheeses and layer cake

MEAT

There is great variety in Scandinavian meat cookery. Meat is not only roasted, stewed, grilled or fried, but it is also made into farce. This is obviously a good way of making your meat go further and a great many dishes are made from farce, the most famous ones being the Danish rissoles, *frikadeller*, and the Swedish meatballs, *köttbullar*. Furthermore, the old tradition of preserving meat by salting or curing it is still practised and many of the best dishes are made from cured pork, lamb or beef, boiled and served with fresh vegetables in season. Meat is cut differently from the way we are used to in this country. The joints are easier to carve and, generally speaking, there seems to be less wastage from the cheaper cuts. The Danes are probably the greatest meat eaters of the three nations; pork and beef are their chief meats, followed by veal and lamb. The last is considered an expensive delicacy, as only spring lamb is served. Veal is delicious and, like the Dutch veal, superior to English, whereas the beef is not as good as the best English or Scottish beef, because the cattle are chiefly raised for their milk. Norway, with its mountainous landscape and severe climate, is naturally more limited in its raising of cattle, and sheep provide the chief source of home-grown meat. *Fenalår*, cured and smoked leg of mutton, is one of the delicacies which visitors to Norway ought to try.

Cured baked or glazed ham is the traditional Christmas fare in Sweden as well as in Norway, where it is served with creamed butter piped over the top (see picture on book jacket). Ham stock or the juices from baked ham are used for what the Swedes call *Dopp i Grytan*, which literally means 'dip in the pan', the idea being that slices of bread are dipped in the heated stock which is placed in the centre of the Christmas table. Veal is very popular in Sweden, often pot-roasted, and lamb is cooked in various delicious ways.

Offal is used a great deal in all Scandinavian countries: kidneys are often served in a cream sauce, for example, and used as a filling in omelettes, as are sweetbreads.

Calf's head is used for the ingenious dish of Mock Turtle, which is elegant enough for any party occasion.

FRIED PORK AND APPLES

D. ÆBLEFLÆSK
N. EPLEFLESK
S. ÄPPELFLÄSK

This dish is probably originally Danish, but it is also known in Sweden, particularly in the southern parts, and in Norway.

Preparation time 10 minutes
Cooking time 20—30 minutes
To serve 3

You will need

1 lb. fresh or slightly salt belly of pork, cut into thin slices
1 lb. cooking apples, cored but not peeled
2 tablespoons brown sugar

Heat the dry frying pan well, and then turn down the heat and fry the pork slices over low heat until crisp, pouring some of the fat out of the frying pan from time to time. Remove the fried pork and keep the slices hot. Slice the apples into thin rings, fry in the pork fat until tender and sprinkle with sugar. Serve at once with fried pork (see photograph page 85).

Preparing stuffed spareribs

Stuffed spareribs with red cabbage and boiled potatoes

GLAZED SMOKED LOIN OF PORK

D. GLASERET HAMBURGERRYG

Preparation time 10 minutes
Cooking time 50 minutes
Oven temperature 375°F. Gas Mark 5
To serve 6

You will need

2—3 lb. smoked loin of pork
scant ½ pint (U.S. 1 cup) red wine
2 bay leaves
sprigs of fresh dill *or*
   1 tablespoon dried dill
8 whole peppercorns
soft brown sugar
mustard powder
butter

Place the pork on a large piece of aluminium foil and put it into an oblong cake tin, long enough and deep enough to hold the meat but no bigger. Pour enough red wine over the meat to cover it. Scatter the bay leaves, dill and peppercorns over the meat and leave to marinate for 2—4 hours. Wrap the foil over the top of the pork. Place the covered meat in the oven and cook for 45 minutes in a moderately hot oven. Leave the meat to cool in the foil.
Before serving, spread brown sugar mixed with dry mustard powder (two-thirds sugar to one-third mustard) on top of the pork, dot with knobs of butter and put into a hot oven to glaze with the door ajar. Serve at once, cut into thick slices with hot vegetables and creamed butter (see recipe page 66 and photograph page 86).

ROAST SPARERIBS STUFFED WITH APPLES AND PRUNES

D. RIBBENSTEG MED ÆBLER OG SVESKER
N. FYLT RIBBE
S. UGNSTEKT REVBENSSPJALL

Preparation time 30 minutes
Cooking time 1¾—2 hours
Oven temperature 350°F. Gas Mark 4
To serve 4—6

You will need

8 oz. prunes
3—4 lb. lean spareribs *or*
   belly of pork
salt and pepper
1 lb. apples
1½ pints (U.S. 3¾ cups) water
seasoning
plain flour
gravy browning (optional)

Wash the prunes and soak them overnight. Remove the stones. Ask your butcher to crack the sparerib bones two or three times across. Trim off any excess fat and season the meat all over with salt and pepper. Peel, core and slice the apples and place these on the meat, together with the prunes. Roll up the meat (as shown in the photograph), tie it with string into a neat shape and place it on a rack in a roasting pan in the oven; leave it to brown before adding the water. Baste the meat from time to time and cook for 1½—1¾ hours in a moderate oven. Strain the juices from the roasting pan into a saucepan and skim off any fat.

Stuffing fillet of pork

Stuffed fillet of pork, shaped and ready for cooking

Season the juices and thicken them while boiling, with a little flour and water stirred to make a thin paste. Add gravy browning if desired and continue to simmer the gravy for 4—5 minutes. Serve hot, with the hot sparerib cut into slices. Red cabbage and glazed potatoes (see pages 109 and 108) are usually served with this dish.

Roast spareribs are also delicious served cold and may very often be found on the smörgåsbord accompanied by apple sauce.

ROAST SPARERIBS

S. UGNSTEKT REVBENSSPJÄLL

Preparation time 15 minutes
Cooking time 1¾—2 hours
Oven temperature 425°F. Gas Mark 7 *then*
                   350°F. Gas Mark 4
To serve 4—6

You will need

3—4 lb. spareribs
½ tablespoon salt
½ teaspoon ground white pepper
¾ teaspoon powdered ginger *or*
   dry mustard
½ oz. butter
½ pint boiling water
½ pint prune juice

Trim off any excess fat and rub the meat with salt, pepper and ginger or mustard. Melt the butter in a heavy cast-iron casserole and brown the meat on both sides in a very hot oven. Reduce the heat and

continue roasting the meat in a moderate oven for about 1½—1¾ hours until tender. Pour the boiling water into the casserole and baste the meat from time to time; finally pour in the prune juice. Strain the juices, skim off the fat and pour into a sauce-boat. Serve with boiled potatoes, apple sauce and cooked prunes.

FRIED FILLET OF PORK

D. MØRBRADBØFFER

Preparation time 6 minutes
Cooking time 6 minutes
To serve 4

You will need

2 fillets of pork (about 1¾ lb.)
plain flour seasoned with salt, pepper and
   mustard, if liked
2 oz. butter

Trim excess fat from the fillets and remove sinews. Cut the fillets crosswise into ¾-inch slices and dip these in the flour. Melt the butter in a frying pan and when it is turning golden brown, fry the pork slices for 2—3 minutes on each side until brown and cooked. Serve with potatoes, either boiled or glazed, and with creamed spinach, red cabbage (see pages 108 and 109) or cranberries.

VARIATION

Fried fillet of pork may also be served either in a mushroom sauce or with crisply fried onion rings (see photograph page 82).

Fried fillet of pork

STUFFED FILLET OF PORK

D. MØRBRAD MED ÆBLER OG SVESKER

Fillet of pork is one of the most versatile cuts of meat. In Scandinavian cooking it is used in a variety of ways: instead of the apple and prune filling described below, it is sometimes stuffed with plain parsley, mushrooms, chopped ham or a farce made from kidneys.

Preparation time 15 minutes
Cooking time 30 minutes
To serve 4

You will need

2 fillets of pork (about 1¾ lb. meat)
1—2 cooking apples, peeled, cored and sliced
8 prunes, previously soaked and stoned
salt
pepper
1½ oz. butter
½—¾ pint (U.S. 1¼—1¾ cups) stock or water
¼—½ pint (U.S. ⅔—1¼ cups) single or double cream
soy sauce or gravy browning

Trim excess fat from the fillets and remove sinews. Cut the fillets halfway through lengthwise, and beat them out gently (see photograph page 81). Place the sliced apples and soaked prunes on the meat; season with salt and pepper and tie up the fillets with pieces of cotton (see photograph page 81). Brown the butter in the heavy casserole and place fillets in this; brown the meat all over and season

with a little salt and pepper. Pour over the stock and cook over gentle heat for about 20 minutes with the lid covering the saucepan. Add the cream and cook for a further 10 minutes, or until the meat is done. Serve the fillets of pork sliced crosswise with the gravy served separately and with potatoes and red cabbage (see page 109).

SAILOR'S STEW 1.

D. SKIPPERLABSKOVS (HVID)

Preparation time 30—40 minutes
Cooking time 2 hours
To serve 4

You will need

1½—2 lb. stewing beef (clod, flank or shin)
approximately 1 pint (U.S. 2½ cups) water
12 oz. onions, cut into rings
1—2 bay leaves
1½ lb. potatoes, cubed
salt to taste
pepper to taste
chopped parsley or chives
knobs of cold butter
chopped smoked ham (optional)

Remove excess fat from meat, cut it into 1 to 2-inch cubes and put it in a saucepan with the water. Bring to the boil and remove any scum which may form. Add the onions and bring to the boil again; remove any further scum. Add the bay leaves, cover with a lid, and continue cooking over low heat for about 1 hour. Add the cubed potatoes and cook until the meat is tender and the potatoes have become so soft that they thicken the gravy, and have the consistency of mashed potatoes. Season with salt and pepper, pour into a serving dish.
Sprinkle with the chopped parsley or chives and top with small knobs of cold butter. Serve the chopped, smoked ham separately, if used, and serve with dark rye bread, lager and snaps.

SAILOR'S STEW 2.

D. SØMANDSTRET
N. SJÖMANNSBIFF
S. SJÖMANSBIFF

Preparation time 45 minutes
Cooking time 1½—1¾ hours
Oven temperature 375°F. Gas Mark 5
To serve 4

You will need

1½—2 lb. chuck steak
2 oz. butter
salt
pepper
12 oz. onions, thinly sliced
1½ lb. potatoes, sliced
scant ¼ pint (U.S. ½ cup) hot water
approximately 1 pint (U.S. 2½ cups) beer
chopped chives or parsley
knobs of cold butter

Cut the meat into slices ¼ inch thick and pound them lightly. Melt the butter in a saucepan with a heavy base and when the butter is turning brown, add the meat. Brown the meat on both sides and season with salt and pepper. Add the onions and sauté these until they are golden coloured and transparent.

Place half the sliced potatoes in a buttered casserole dish and layer the meat and onions on top; cover with the remaining half of the sliced potatoes and sprinkle with a little more salt and pepper.

Pour the hot water into the saucepan in which the meat and onions were cooked, bring it to the boil and scrape the juices into the casserole over the potatoes and the meat; add the beer, cover the casserole with a tight-fitting lid and cook the stew in a fairly hot oven for 1—1½ hours until the meat is tender. Serve sprinkled with chopped chives or parsley and small knobs of cold butter on top (see photograph page 90).

BEEF À LA LINDSTRÖM

S. BIFF A LA LINDSTRÖM

Preparation time 15 minutes
Cooking time   10 minutes
To serve   4

You will need

1¼ lb. minced beef
2 boiled potatoes, mashed
2 egg yolks
6—8 tablespoons single cream
2 pickled beetroots (see page 32), finely diced
1½ tablespoons finely chopped onion
2 tablespoons finely chopped capers
salt
pinch ground white pepper
pinch paprika pepper
3 oz. butter

Mix the minced beef with the mashed potatoes and egg yolks, and gradually stir in the cream. Add the beetroot, onion and capers; stir carefully and season with salt, paprika and white pepper. Shape into round, flat cakes about 1 inch thick and fry in hot butter over a medium heat for 3—4 minutes on each side. Serve hot with fresh vegetables.

Burning passion

MOCK TURTLE

D. FORLOREN SKILDPADDE

Preparation time 3 hours
Cooking time 4½ hours
To serve 12

You will need

1 calf's head
water
salt
bouquet garni
4 oz. butter
4 medium-sized onions, sliced
2 leeks, white parts only, sliced
4 carrots, sliced
1 celeriac, peeled and cubed
2 oz. butter
4 tablespoons plain flour
paprika to taste
lemon juice to taste
¼ pint (U.S. ⅔ cup) Madeira
10 oz. fish balls (see page 74)
10 oz. small meat balls (see page 90)
Brain balls (optional, see page 66)
6 Smiling Eggs (see page 52)

Have calf's head split into halves and the brain removed. Keep the brains for making brain balls if desired, and reserve the tongue. Discard the eyes and ears, brush the head well with a stiff brush before rinsing it in several lots of cold water. Leave the calf's head to soak in cold water for about 6 hours. Remove the calf's head and scald it again. Place in a saucepan with just sufficient water to cover it, add the salt and bouquet garni. Bring slowly to the boil and remove any scum which forms. Simmer for about three hours until tender, drain the calf's head and preserve the stock. Remove the meat from the bone and cut into 1-inch cubes. Press the cubed meat between two plates with a heavy weight on top. Cook the tongue separately until tender; drain, cool and skin and cut it into 1-inch cubes. Brown 4 oz. of the butter in a saucepan; add the prepared vegetables and sauté them for a few minutes. Add about 3 pints of the stock from the calf's head. Simmer for about 1—1½ hours and strain. Melt the remaining butter in a saucepan with a heavy base and stir in the flour. Cook the butter and flour until nutty brown, then gradually stir in the strained stock. Cook over low heat until smooth and thick. Season with paprika, lemon juice and Madeira. Add the cubed calf's meat, including the cubed tongue, the fish balls, meat balls and brain balls and heat carefully, without boiling, until hot. Serve hot in deep plates garnished with halved Smiling Eggs (see page 52).

Have extra Madeira ready on the table to add to the dish if desired. Serve with hot French bread or puff pastry triangles (see page 134).

MOCK HARE

D. FORLOREN HARE

This very popular dish is really a meat loaf. The gravy is a typical example of gravy for real game dishes.

Preparation time 20 minutes
Cooking time 30—35 minutes
Oven temperature 400°F. Gas Mark 6
To serve 4—6

You will need

9 oz. minced veal
9 oz. minced pork
2½ oz. toasted brown breadcrumbs
2 eggs
1—2 teaspoons salt
3 tablespoons single cream
4 oz. smoked back fat of pork, cut into ½-inch squares
2 oz. butter
6—8 tablespoons stock
scant ¾ pint (U.S. 1¾ cups) milk *or* equal quantities of milk and cream
1½ oz. plain flour
salt
pepper
soy sauce
redcurrant jelly

Mix the minced veal, minced pork and brown breadcrumbs. Stir in the eggs one at a time. Season with salt and pepper and finally stir in the single cream. Beat the mixture for a few minutes; mould the meat into an oblong 'hare' shape in the roasting pan and lard the meat all along the top with the pieces of back fat of pork (see photograph page 95). Dot with knobs of butter and place in a fairly hot oven to brown. After approximately 10 minutes, when the meat should be nicely brown on top, pour the stock and the milk over the 'hare' and continue to cook for a further 20 minutes. Pour the juices from the pan into a saucepan and bring to the boil. Thicken with the flour (mixed with water to a thin paste); season with salt and pepper and add a little soy sauce to colour the gravy.
Finally, add redcurrant jelly to taste. Serve with apple halves filled with redcurrant jelly, glazed potatoes and red cabbage (see pages 96, 108 and 109).

Smoked buckling omelette and fried pork and apples

Glazed smoked loin of pork with vegetables and cream butter

86

Asparagus wrapped in pickled salmon and meat rissoles

Veal casserole

BURNING PASSION

D. BRÆNDENDE KÆRLIGHED

This is a good old Danish country dish which ought to be included, if only because of its name.

Preparation time 15 minutes
Cooking time   30 minutes
To serve   4

You will need

4 medium-sized onions, sliced
butter
6—8 oz. salt or fresh streaky pork diced *or*
    6—8 oz. streaky bacon, diced
hot mashed potatoes (made from 2 lb.
    potatoes)
pickled beetroot (see page 32), diced

Fry the sliced onions in the butter until golden and crisp. Remove them from the frying pan, retaining the butter for use later, and keep them hot. Fry the diced pork until crisp and brown, in the hot fat in which the onions were cooked. Pile or pipe the mashed potatoes into a hot serving dish; place the cooked pork down the centre of the dish and garnish with diced beetroot all round the edges of the dish. Pile the fried onions on top (see photograph page 83).

VEAL CASSEROLE

D. GRYDERET MED KALVEKØD

Preparation time 30 minutes
Cooking time   1 hour
To serve   4

You will need

1¾ lb. stewing veal
2—3 oz. butter
2 large onions, finely chopped
salt
pepper
paprika
pinch of fresh or dried thyme
bouquet garni
½ pint (U.S. 1¼ cups) stock
8 oz. mushrooms, trimmed and sliced
cornflour
chopped parsley

Cut the meat into cubes and fry them in browned butter in a heavy-based saucepan. Add the onions and cook until golden brown. Season with salt, pepper and paprika and add the thyme and the bouquet garni. Pour in the stock and cook, covered with a lid, over low heat for about 1 hour or until the meat is tender. Add the mushrooms and continue to cook for 5 minutes. Thicken the gravy with a little cornflour, mixed to a thin paste with a little cold water, and add to the boiling gravy. Cook for a further 3—4 minutes. Garnish with parsley and serve with boiled rice or new potatoes (see photograph page 88).

MINCED BEEFSTEAK WITH SOFT ONIONS

D. HAKKEBØF MED LØG

Choose only the best juicy, freshly-minced beef for this Danish Hamburger recipe. Have the beef minced once or twice. Serve the beefsteaks with onions, as described below, or with crisply fried onions. In Denmark, a fried egg is often served on top of each beefsteak.

Preparation time 30 minutes
Cooking time   15—20 minutes
To serve   4

You will need

1 lb. onions, sliced
5—6 oz. butter
3 tablespoons water
2 lb. minced beef
seasoned flour
generous ½ pint (U.S. 1½ cups) stock

Fry the onions in 2 oz. of the hot butter, until they are turning brown; add the water and continue to cook until it has evaporated. Put the onions on a plate and keep them hot. Shape the beef into round, flat hamburgers about 1 inch thick, and dip these in the seasoned flour. Melt the remaining butter in the frying pan, and when it is turning brown fry the hamburgers in it for 3—4 minutes on each side. The meat should be nicely brown on the outside and pink inside. Arrange the cooked hamburgers on a serving dish and pile the fried onions on top. Pour the stock into the butter in the frying pan and bring to the boil. Season and serve with the hamburgers. New potatoes and pickled beetroot (see page 32) go well with this dish.

FARCE (FORCEMEAT) 1.

D. FARS
N. KJÖTTDEIG

Farce is widely used in a variety of Scandinavian dishes, the most popular ones probably being the Swedish meatballs and the Danish rissoles. There are perhaps almost as many ways of making farce as there are housewives in Scandinavia, but there are a few general rules that must be adhered to which distinguish the Scandinavian farce from its English counterpart. It may be made from either one type of meat or a mixture of two. The meat must be free from all sinews and should be neither too fat nor too lean. It may be minced up to ten times, depending on how fine you like your farce to be, though 4—5 times should be sufficient to suit most people's taste. The most important part in the making of farce is, however, the stirring or rather beating of it. If you have an electric mixer this is easy, if not, do what housewives used to do before its invention—beat the meat well, each time you pass it. Only if you beat the farce well, will it become aerated and of the correct light texture.

Preparation time 30 minutes

You will need

8 oz. lean pork, minced
8 oz. veal or beef, minced
1½ teaspoons salt
pinch ground white pepper
pinch ground allspice, nutmeg or ground
   cloves
1 egg or 2 egg whites
3 tablespoons plain flour
½—¾ pint (U.S. 1¼—1¾ cups) soda water *or*
   equal quantities of water and single cream
1 small onion, grated

Mix the pork and veal with the seasonings and spices, in a basin; stir in the lightly beaten egg, or whites. Mix the flour with the liquid to make a thin paste and add this gradually to the meat mixture; finally add the grated onion. Beat the mixture extremely well. Leave the farce in a cold place for about 1 hour before using it. Always cook one or two meat balls first, to see if spices should be adjusted, and if the farce is of the right consistency. If the mixture has become too stiff, add a little more liquid. As you can see from the following recipes, a number of dishes can be made with farce. A farce mixture should always be cooked the day that it is made.

Sailor's stew

Forcemeat mould

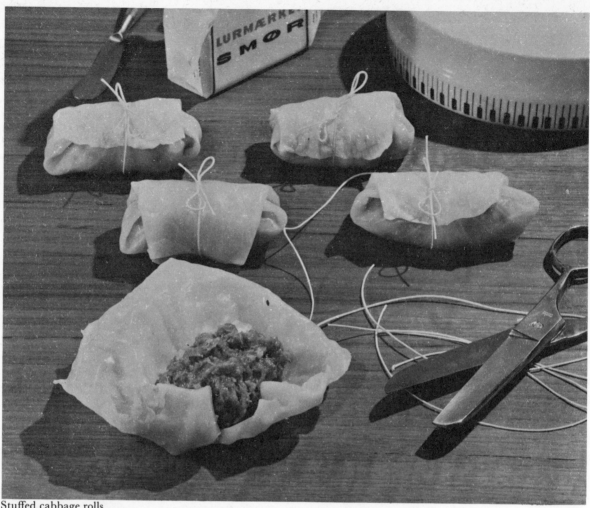

Stuffed cabbage rolls

FARCE (FORCEMEAT) 2.

D. FARS
N. KJÖTTDEIG

Preparation time 30 minutes

You will need

1 lb. minced beef or equal quantities of pork
   and veal, minced
approximately 1 oz. plain flour
approximately 1 oz. potato flour
3 oz. water
12 fl. oz. (U.S. 1½ cups) single cream or milk
1½ teaspoons salt
pinch pepper

Mix the meat with the flour and gradually stir in
the water followed by the cream. Season with salt
and pepper and proceed as for recipe for farce 1 (see
page 90).

MEAT RISSOLES

D. FRIKADELLER
N. KJÖTTBOLLER

Preparation time 1¼ hours
Cooking time   10—12 minutes
To serve   4

You will need

3—4 oz. butter
farce (see page 90)

Brown the butter in a frying pan. Shape the farce
into oval or round balls with two wet spoons. Fry
the rissoles in the browned butter for about 5
minutes on each side. Shake the frying pan so that
they brown all over. Make sure the rissoles are
cooked thoroughly. Serve with potatoes, fresh
vegetables and hot, melted butter. Red cabbage
goes well with this dish (see recipe page 109 and
photograph page 87).

STUFFED CABBAGE ROLLS

D. KÅLROULETTER
N. KÅLRULETTER
S. KÅLDOLMAR

This would seem to be a homely Scandinavian version of the stuffed vine leaves which the Turks and the Greeks call dolmas.

Preparation time 1 hour
Cooking time 35 minutes
To serve 4—6

You will need

1 white cabbage
farce (see page 90)
salt water
4 oz. butter (optional)

Remove 10—12 of the large outer leaves of the cabbage and rinse them. Boil the leaves in salted water for 2 minutes, drain and pat dry with absorbent paper. Spread about 1—2 tablespoons of farce on each leaf, fold in the ends of the leaves to prevent the stuffing from slipping out during the cooking, roll each leaf into a little parcel and tie it with thin cotton (see photograph page 92). Boil the stuffed cabbage leaves in salted water for 20—30 minutes, according to their size. Serve hot with tomato sauce, or brown the cabbage rolls in butter after they have been cooked, and serve with extra hot browned butter.
Note
Cooked rice may be added to the farce.

FORCEMEAT MOULD

D. KØDFARSRAND
N. KJÖTTPUDDING

Preparation time 1½ hour
Cooking time 30—45 minutes
To serve 4

You will need

farce (see page 90)

The farce should not be too stiff for this dish. Butter a mould, preferably ring-shaped, and place the farce in this. Cover the mould with a lid or greaseproof paper, and place it on a rack in a saucepan. Pour boiling water into the saucepan until it reaches half-way up the sides of the mould. Cover the saucepan with a lid and cook the mould in the boiling water for 30—45 minutes over gentle heat. Make sure the water does not boil fiercely or it will boil over into the mould.
Unmould out on to a hot serving dish and fill the centre with cooked vegetables (see photograph page 91). Creamed Butter (see page 66) or hot butter should be served with this dish.

MEAT BALLS IN CELERIAC SAUCE

D. KØDBOLLER I SELLERI

Preparation time 1½ hours
Cooking time 30 minutes
To serve 4—6

You will need

1 large celeriac (weighing about 1 lb.)
water
farce (see page 90)
generous pint (U.S. generous 2½ cups) of stock from celeriac
1½ oz. butter
1½ oz. plain flour
1 or 2 egg yolks
salt and pepper

Peel and dice the celeriac and boil it until tender. Strain the liquid into a clean saucepan and reserve the celeriac. Shape the farce into small balls; bring the celeriac stock to the boil and drop the farce balls into it. Cook over very low heat for a few minutes until the balls are firm and cooked. Remove them from the stock with a slotted spoon. Melt the butter and add the flour; stir for a few minutes over gentle heat. Gradually whisk in about 1 pint of the hot celeriac stock and continue to cook over low heat, until the sauce is smooth and thick. Add the cooked, diced celeriac and meat balls; allow to heat through gently. Beat the egg yolks with a little of the hot sauce and a dash of salt and pepper, stir the egg mixture into the hot sauce. Remove saucepan from heat and serve at once. Serve with French bread.

STUFFED CABBAGE

D. FARSERET KÅL

Preparation time 1¼ hours
Cooking time 2 hours
To serve 6

You will need

farce (see page 90)
1 large white cabbage
boiling water

Trim the outside leaves from the white cabbage and cut off a slice from the base of the cabbage. Hollow out the cabbage with a sharp knife, leaving a shell about ¾ inch thick. Cook the part which you have cut out separately. Spoon the forcemeat into the hollow in the cabbage, replace the 'lid' on this and either wrap the cabbage in a clean muslin or linen cloth or tie it securely with thin string or cotton. Place the stuffed cabbage in gently boiling water, and cook it for about 2 hours with a lid on the saucepan. Serve with melted butter or Cream Horseradish Sauce (see page 68).

SWEDISH FARCE (FORCEMEAT)

S. KÖTTFARS

Preparation time 30 minutes

You will need

1 tablespoon grated or chopped onion
½ oz. butter
7 tablespoons dried white breadcrumbs
½ pint milk or cream and water
1 lb. minced beef and 4 oz. minced pork *or*
   12 oz. minced beef and 4 oz. each minced
   veal and pork
salt
white pepper
pinch allspice (optional)
1 egg

Sauté the onion in the butter until golden brown. Soak the breadcrumbs in the liquid. Mix the minced meat with the seasonings, and stir in the egg and the fried onion. Add the soaked breadcrumbs and the liquid and beat the farce until it is smooth. Use for small meat balls for the smörgåsbord or for larger balls served in gravy as a dinner dish (see next column), or for any of the other recipes using farce.

SWEDISH MEATBALLS

S. KÖTTBULLAR

Preparation time 40 minutes
Cooking time 25 minutes

You will need

Swedish meat farce (see this page)
butter for frying

Shape the farce into small balls, using two teaspoons dipped in cold water. Heat the butter in a frying pan and fry a few meat balls at a time for 3—5 minutes. Shake the pan so that the balls brown all over and continue to fry over gentle heat, without a lid. Lift out the meat balls and serve either hot or cold on the smörgåsbord.
Note
If the meat balls are to be served with gravy or sauce as a supper dish, shape the farce into larger sizes and fry for 5—8 minutes. Remove the meat balls to a hot platter and keep them hot; meanwhile swirl out the pan with approximately ¾ pint stock and add about 2 tablespoons of thick cream. The sauce may be thickened more with a little flour or cornflour added to the boiling sauce. Taste and season the gravy before serving it separately.

CREAMED SWEETBREADS

D. BRISSELSTUVNING
N. BRISSELSTUING
S. KALVBRÄSSTUVNING

Calves' sweetbreads are considered to be the most delicious, but lambs' sweetbreads which are considerably cheaper may also be used.

Preparation time 15—20 minutes
Cooking time 30 minutes
To serve 4—6

You will need

1 lb. calves' sweetbreads
2 oz. butter
1¾ oz. plain flour
½ pint stock from sweetbreads
salt
pepper
lemon juice to taste
generous ½ pint single or double cream

Soak the sweetbreads in cold water for 1—2 hours. Clean and remove as many of the blood vessels as possible. Blanch the sweetbreads by placing them in a saucepan and covering with cold water. Add salt and lemon juice, bring to the boil and simmer for about 15 minutes. Drain, reserving ½ pint of the liquid, and plunge into cold water for 5 minutes. Remove membranes and place sweetbreads on a plate with a light weight on top. When they are completely cold, dice them. Melt the butter in a saucepan and add the flour. Gradually add the stock from the cooked sweetbreads, season with salt, pepper and lemon juice. Finally, stir in the cream. Cook until smooth. Add the diced sweetbreads, heat through and serve as a filling in omelettes or in pastry shells or with a spinach ring (see pages 144 and 52).

VARIATION

After making the sauce, stir in 8 oz. sliced, fresh mushrooms and allow them to cook in the sauce for 10 minutes. Then proceed with the recipe.

Mock hare with poached apple halves

POACHED APPLE HALVES

D. HALVE KOGTE ÆBLER

Preparation time 10 minutes
Cooking time 5 minutes
To serve 4—6

You will need

4 medium-sized cooking apples
4 oz. sugar
scant ½ pint water
redcurrant jelly

Peel and halve the apples. Remove the cores and place them in water with a little lemon juice or vinegar to prevent discolouration. Bring sugar and water to the boil in a saucepan. Lower the heat and place the apple halves gently in the boiling syrup, a few at a time, only. Simmer for approximately 5 minutes, or until the apples are tender. Do not over-cook them or they will break. Carefully lift out the apple halves, with a slotted spoon, and leave to drain before filling the hollow of each with a spoon-ful of redcurrant jelly. Serve as a garnish with mock hare (see photograph page 95), game, roast duck, roast goose or roast pork.

LAMB AND CABBAGE

D. FÅR I KÅL
N. FÅRIKÅL
S. FÅR I KÅL

Preparation time 25 minutes
Cooking time 1—1½ hours
To serve 4

You will need

2—2½ lb. shoulder or breast of lamb or
    mutton
1 small cabbage
1 teaspoon salt
10 black peppercorns
1 bay leaf
½—¾ pint (1¼—2 cups) water
finely chopped parsley

Trim and cut the meat into large, even-sized cubes and then blanch in boiling water. Remove some of the outer, coarse leaves of the cabbage and cut the stalk away. Make layers of cabbage and meat in a heavy casserole. Sprinkle with salt and peppercorns between layers. Add the bay leaf and sufficient water to cover the ingredients. Bring to the boil and skim the surface well; turn down the heat and cover with a lid. Simmer on top of the cooker or bake in a moderate to fairly hot oven for about 1—1½ hours until the meat is tender. Just before serving sprinkle with parsley. Serve with hot French bread or dark Danish rye bread.

LAMB AND ASPARAGUS

D. LAM I ASPARGES

This is a delicious dish when made with fresh young asparagus—white or green. Canned asparagus may also be used, but it remains a second best.

Preparation time 15—20 minutes
Cooking time 1¾—2 hours
To serve 4—6

You will need

2—3 lb. shoulder of lamb
water
pinch salt
¾—1 lb. fresh asparagus
2 oz. butter
2 oz. flour
2 egg yolks *or*
    2 tablespoons double cream (optional)

Place the lamb in a saucepan and cover it with cold water. Bring to boil and skim. Lower the heat, add the salt and cook, covered with a lid, for about 1½ hours until the meat is almost tender. Prepare the asparagus, reserving the peel and woody ends which have been trimmed off. Wrap these in a piece of muslin and add to the lamb, together with the pre-pared asparagus. Cook for 20 minutes until the asparagus is tender. (If canned asparagus is used, add it to the lamb a few minutes before the end of the cooking time). Remove the asparagus, drain and keep hot. Discard the muslin bag and remove the saucepan from the heat. In a second saucepan melt the butter and add the flour; cook for 1—2 minutes and gradually add about 1¼ pints of the hot liquid from the lamb, stirring all the time. Cook the sauce for 3—5 minutes over gentle heat. Meanwhile, cut the lamb into slices; place these on a hot serving dish and arrange the asparagus on top. The sauce may be further enriched and thickened, either by adding 2 egg yolks stirred with a little of the hot sauce at the last minute, or with a couple of table-spoons of double cream. Pour the hot sauce over the meat and asparagus and serve at once. Hot French bread should be the only accompaniment to this dish.
Note
Shoulder of veal may be cooked in the same way.

Spring chicken with cream gravy and cucumber salad

Roast beef with glazed onions

SCANDINAVIAN HASH

D. BIKSEMAD
N. PYTT I PANNE
S. PYTT I PANNA

I admit I do not find the English name on which I
have decided for this dish, nearly as attractive or
endearing as the Scandinavian ones. The dish has
a certain similarity to the English 'bubble and
squeak', but differs from this because it also contains fried meat. It is, in fact, an excellent way of
using left-over meat and is a great favourite in all
three Scandinavian countries. It even figures on the
menus of many restaurants, particularly at lunch
time. It is usually served with fried eggs and tomato
ketchup, Worcestershire sauce or any other hot-
flavoured sauce.

Preparation time 15 minutes
Cooking time   15—20 minutes
To serve   4

You will need

3 oz. butter
2 medium-sized onions, sliced or chopped
1½ lb. cold boiled *or* canned potatoes, diced
1 lb. cold, cooked meat, diced
salt
pepper

Melt half the butter in a frying pan and sauté the
onions until golden brown. Put the onions on a
plate and keep them hot. Add the remaining
butter to the pan and sauté the potatoes until
they begin to turn brown. Add the meat and cook
for a further 2—3 minutes. Add the sautéed onions
to the pan, season with salt and pepper and heat
through before serving.

Roast Hare with white sauce and garnished with apples and red currant jelly

POULTRY AND GAME

Chicken is usually pot roasted rather than oven roasted; this method ensures that the meat becomes less dry. There are many delicious ways of cooking chicken, for example, in various sauces such as curry, mushroom, horseradish or asparagus and prawn or shrimp.

Spring chicken—not the really tiny poussins, which have hardly any meat on them—stuffed with parsley and cooked with a cream gravy, is one of the great traditional dishes of Scandinavian cooking. Ducks and geese—the traditional Christmas birds—are usually stuffed with apples and prunes and are roasted. They may also be salted and are then equally good served hot or cold. Pigeons used to be found quite often on the menu, but they seem, unfortunately, to be scarcer now. The best season to buy them is late summer and autumn when you are more likely to get a really young pigeon. If they are really young and tender they may be pot roasted or salted and boiled.

Game birds, such as pheasants, partridges and wild ducks, are *barded* to prevent the meat from becoming too dry as well as to add flavour to the dish: thin slices of hard back-fat of pork, either fresh, slightly salted or smoked (failing this, slices of bacon) are tied over the breast of the bird. Game such as reindeer, venison and hare used to be *larded*: *lardoons*—quarter-inch thick strips of the pork fat—were pulled with the aid of a larding needle through the meat along the muscle fibre—a service usually provided by the butcher—but modern Scandinavian cooking tends to apply the barding method in preference to that of larding. The distinctive flavour of the rich gravy which results from this method of cooking, with the addition of cream and redcurrant jelly, adds the finishing Scandinavian touch.

ROAST DUCK

D. STEGT AND

Duck may be stuffed and roasted in the same manner as roast goose (see page 102). Allow approximately 1½ hours for the cooking.

Be wary of the frozen ducks, which always look deceptively bigger whilst still frozen, and also of the so-called ducklings, which sometimes are so small that they are hardly worth the money. A good duck should not be too fat, but should, on the other hand, preferably weigh about 4½—5 lb. ready for the oven. We say in Denmark that a duck is too much for one person, but not enough for two! This may be a slight exaggeration but it is true that a duck is never a very meaty bird. Allow two ducks for four people, using the same amount of stuffing as for the roast goose (see page 102).

SALT GOOSE

D. SPRÆNGT GÅS
N. SPENGT GÅS
S. SPRÅNGD GÅS

Preparation time 25 minutes
Cooking time 2—2½ hours
To serve 8

You will need

4½ oz. salt
1½ oz. sugar
scant oz. saltpetre
1 goose (about 9 lb. when cleaned)
2 pieces of lump sugar
3—4 black peppercorns
1 bouquet garni
1 small onion, peeled

Mix the salt, sugar and saltpetre and rub the goose inside and outside with this mixture. Place the goose in a glazed crock and leave in a cold place for 48—72 hours. Reserve the giblets, storing them in the refrigerator until required. From time to time, spoon over the salt mixture which has collected at the bottom of the crock. Take out the goose, rinse it in tepid water and place it in a saucepan, breast side up. Pour sufficient boiling water over, to cover it. Bring quickly to the boil, skim well and add the lump sugar, whole peppercorns, bouquet garni and the whole onion, and also the giblets, with the exception of the liver, which may be used for a pâté. Simmer for 2—2½ hours, until the goose is tender. Serve hot with melted butter or cold horseradish cream sauce (see page 68) and cooked vegetables in season: white and green asparagus, yellow butter and the delicate shades of pink meat would make this dish a feast for the eye as well as the palate.

Alternatively, use the stock for yellow pea soup (see pages 63 and 64) and serve the goose with or without the streaky pork which usually accompanies the soup. If the goose is to be served cold, leave it to cool down in the cooling liquor and serve it with cold potato salad 1 or 2 (see page 28) or small glazed onions (see page 110), cold horseradish cream sauce (see page 68) and watercress.

VARIATION

Salt duck, known in Denmark as Sprængt And, may be cooked and served in the same way: use half quantities of salt, sugar and saltpetre for 1 duck weighing about 4½ lb. The cooking time is 1½ hours or until the duck is tender.

ROAST GOOSE WITH APPLES AND PRUNES

D. GÅSESTEG MED ÆBLER OG SVESKER
N. STEKT GÅS FYLT MED FRUKT
S. STEKT GÅS MED FRUKTFYLLNING

The goose is the traditional Christmas bird, eaten on Christmas Eve in Denmark, though some families prefer duck or roast pork. The apple and prune stuffing makes an excellent accompaniment for the rather fat meat of the goose. Make sure your goose is a young one, or it will be tough! Choose a bird which weighs less than 10 lb. You can cook the goose either slowly or by the ordinary shorter method described below.

Preparation time 35 minutes
Cooking time 3 hours
Oven temperature 400°F. Gas Mark 6
To serve 8

You will need

8 oz. prunes
water
9 lb. goose
½ lemon
salt
pepper
4 medium-sized cooking apples, peeled, cored and sliced
2 pints (U.S. 5 cups) boiling stock or water
salt and pepper to taste
plain flour
water
gravy browning or soy sauce

Rinse the prunes, soak them overnight and remove the stones. Clean the goose and remove and keep any excess fat. Rub the goose inside and outside with lemon, salt and pepper. Stuff the bird with prunes and apples, sew or skewer the opening together, and truss the bird in the usual manner. Prick the skin lightly with a fork all over, to allow excess fat to escape during roasting. Place the goose on its side on a meat rack in the roasting pan in a moderately hot to hot oven. After 30 minutes, pour off the fat which has accumulated in the pan—do not discard it, but keep it for dripping (see page 33). Pour the boiling stock into the roasting pan and continue cooking, basting the goose from time to time. After 1½ hours turn the goose on to the other side and cook for a further 1½ hours. 30 minutes before the goose is done, pour off the juices from the roasting pan into a saucepan; leave to cool down and skim off the fat. During the last 5—10 minutes of the cooking leave the oven door ajar so that the skin of the goose becomes crisp. Alternatively, spoon over several tablespoons of cold water and continue to cook with the oven door closed for 15 minutes. Meanwhile, make the gravy from the juices by thickening with flour stirred to a thin paste with a little cold water and added to the boiling juices. Season with salt and pepper and colour with gravy browning or soy sauce. Boil gently for 2—3 minutes whilst stirring and leave to simmer for a further 5 minutes before serving separately. Serve with hot red cabbage and glazed potatoes (see recipes pages 108 and 109 and photograph page 135).

CHICKEN IN ASPARAGUS AND PRAWN SAUCE

D. HØNS I ASPARGES OG REJER

Preparation time 30 minutes
Cooking time 1½ hours
To serve 4

You will need

3—4 lb. chicken, quartered
1½—2 pints (U.S. 3¾—5 cups) water
bouquet garni
salt
2 oz. butter
1½ oz. plain flour
1 lb. cooked asparagus (fresh or canned)
generous ¼ pint (U.S. ¾ cup) asparagus stock
4 oz. cooked, peeled prawns
2 large egg yolks
salt

Place the chicken quarters in a saucepan with about 2 pints of water and bring slowly to the boil. Skim and add the bouquet garni and salt. Continue to simmer over a low heat, with the lid on, until the chicken pieces are tender—about 1 hour. Remove the chicken pieces and keep them hot.
Melt the butter in another saucepan and add the flour. Stir until smooth and gradually add the hot chicken and asparagus stock, stir all the time, over low heat. Allow the white sauce to boil for a few minutes, add the chicken pieces to the sauce together with the asparagus and prawns, and heat gently for a few more minutes without boiling. Stir the egg yolks and salt with a little of the warm sauce, in a cup. Remove the saucepan from the heat and add the egg yolks to the sauce. Serve accompanied by hot French bread and a green salad to follow.

SPRING CHICKEN WITH CREAM GRAVY

D. STEGT KYLLING MED SKILT SAUCE
S. STEKT KYCKLING MED GRÄDDSÅS

There is a lot to be said for cooking chickens in a casserole or Dutch oven, rather than roasting them, as roasting tends to make the meat dry. This applies particularly to the frozen birds we often buy today. This recipe is a favourite one amongst the Danes, especially on account of its rich, creamy gravy.

Preparation time 30 minutes
Cooking time 45 minutes
To serve 4

You will need

2 spring chickens, cleaned and ready for cooking
salt
pepper
bunch parsley, washed and stalks removed
6—7 oz. butter
1 pint (U.S. 2½ cups) single cream *or* equal quantities single and double cream

Rub the chickens with salt and pepper both inside and outside. Chop the parsley coarsely and combine it with about one-third of the butter. Stuff the chickens with this butter and parsley mixture and truss in the usual way.
Melt the remaining butter in a casserole with a heavy base; when it has turned a nutty brown colour, fry the chickens until they are evenly brown all over. Add the giblets and lower the heat. Partly cover the casserole with a lid and continue to cook for 30—45 minutes, according to the size of the birds. Just before serving, add the cream and simmer for 3—4 minutes, until the cream coagulates and the juices separate. This special sauce is called 'Skilt Sauce' in Danish. In spite of its rather strange appearance, it is delicious, being both rich and creamy.
Serve the chickens cut in half, accompanied with either boiled or glazed potatoes—or both if preferred—together with either a green or cucumber salad (see recipes pages 108 and 30 and photograph page 97).

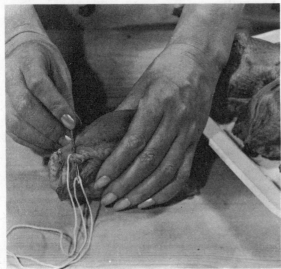

Preparing the pigeons

Sewing up the pigeons after stuffing

Stuffed pigeons

STUFFED PIGEONS

D. FARSEREDE DUER

You will need truly young pigeons for this recipe. If you suspect the age of your pigeons always boil them first before roasting them, or use them in a stewing recipe where they may cook for several hours.

Preparation time 30—40 minutes
Cooking time approximately 1 hour
To serve 4

You will need

4 young pigeons, cleaned and ready for
 cooking
1 small fillet of pork, sinews removed
1 large egg
salt
pepper
pinch thyme
pinch fennel
2 oz. butter
$\frac{1}{2}$—$\frac{3}{4}$ lb. white grapes, skinned
pastry shells or tartlets (see pages 144 and 138)

Remove the breast bone of the pigeons by pressing your thumb and forefinger on either side of the bone (see photograph). Put the pigeon hearts, livers and crops together with the fillet of pork through a mincer, once or twice. Add the egg and stir in the salt, pepper, thyme and fennel. Beat the forcemeat and spoon this into the 4 pigeons. Sew the openings together and truss the birds as shown in the picture. Brown the butter in a heavy casserole and add the pigeons; sprinkle with a little salt, cover with a lid and roast over gentle heat for approximately 1 hour. Ten minutes before the pigeons are done, add the grapes. Remove the pigeons, halve them and place them on a hot serving dish. Spoon the grapes into tartlets and arrange these on the serving dish. Pour the hot buttery juices over the pigeons and serve immediately, accompanied by creamed spinach (see page 109) and potato crisps.
Note
Partridges may be cooked in the same way.

ROAST OR MARINATED VENISON

Venison may be cooked as roast hare or as roast marinated hare (see page 105). The loin is the most tender part of venison and is usually just roasted. The haunch, on the other hand, usually needs a bit of tenderising and it is therefore recommended that this should be marinated before roasting.

ROAST MARINATED HARE

D. MARINERET STEGT HARE
N. MARINERT STEKT HARE
S. MARINERAD STEKT HARE

Preparation time 25—30 minutes
Cooking time 1¼—1¾ hours
Oven temperature 425°F. Gas Mark 7
then 350°F. Gas Mark 4
To serve 6

You will need

1 hare (about 4—5 lb. drawn)

FOR THE MARINADE
1 bottle red wine
1—2 bay leaves
5 allspice, crushed
3—4 juniper berries, crushed
1 teaspoon thyme

Mix the ingredients for the marinade and soak the hare in this, making sure that the marinade completely covers the meat, for at least 36—48 hours. Remove the hare and dry it in a clean cloth. Cook as for roast hare (see opposite), allowing a shorter time. Baste the hare, from time to time, with the marinade in which it has been soaked. Serve with mashed or baked potatoes and plenty of fresh watercress, and with the slightly thickened marinade served separately.

ROAST HARE

D. HARESTEG
N. STEKT HARE
S. STEKT HARE

Preparation time 20—25 minutes
Cooking time 1½—2 hours
Oven temperature 425°F. Gas Mark 7 then 350°F. Gas Mark 4
To serve 6

You will need

4—5 lb. hare, drawn
4 oz. hard back fat of pork or fat bacon
1—1½ oz. butter
1 onion
2 carrots
approximately 1 pint (U.S. 2½ cups) boiling water
1 pint (U.S. 2½ cups) single or double cream *or* 1 pint white sauce
salt and pepper
approximately 1 tablespoon redcurrant jelly

Bard or lard the hare with fat (see page 101). Season with salt and pepper and put small knobs of butter over the top. Put the hare in a hot oven to brown for 10—15 minutes. When evenly brown, reduce the heat to moderate, add the onion and carrots to the roasting tin and pour the boiling water over the hare. Continue to cook until almost done (about 1¼ hours); add the cream or white sauce and cook for a further 15—20 minutes. Strain the sauce into a saucepan and add seasoning and redcurrant jelly to taste. Serve the hot gravy separately, serve with boiled and/or glazed potatoes, red cabbage and/or poached halved apples (see recipes pages 108, 109 and 96 and photograph page 100).

A typical choice of vegetables often used in Scandinavia

VEGETABLES

The idea of 'meat and two vegetables' is not a feature of everyday Scandinavian cooking. Whilst potatoes are served with most dishes they are, more often than not, the only vegetable accompanied simply by pickled beetroot, gherkins, cucumber salad or cranberries. The Scandinavian fondness for potatoes is more easily understood when one realises that a wide choice is available all the year round. It is possible, even in winter, to get small, firm, waxy potatoes, suitable for serving either plainly boiled, glazed or in potato salads. Apart from potatoes, cabbage, leeks and root vegetables, such as carrots and celeriac, are the mainstay during the long winter season. But, for a treasured period in the summer, the thick, snow-white asparagus can be had, together with peas, beans and salad stuff: a purely vegetarian dish of assorted fresh vegetables, served with creamed or melted butter and a sprinkling of herbs, is then a favourite dish. Indeed the grouping of vegetables chosen for their contrast in texture and flavour, as well as colour, is a distinctive feature of Scandinavian cooking, whether they are served on their own or surrounding the meat on a large serving dish (see the Glazed Loin of Pork on page 86). Mention should also be made of the generous use of herbs, particularly the milder varieties, such as dill, chives, parsley and chervil—both in cooking and as decorative garnishes. The Danes use chervil for a delicious summer soup; dill is much favoured for fish dishes, especially in Sweden, and parsley is the most versatile of all.

SWEDISH BAKED POTATOES

S. HASSELBACKSPOTATIS

Preparation time 15 minutes
Cooking time 1 hour
Oven temperature 425°F. Gas Mark 7
To serve 4

You will need

8 medium-sized potatoes, peeled
1½ oz. butter
1½ teaspoon salt
1½ oz. grated Parmesan *or* other cooking cheese
2 tablespoons brown breadcrumbs

Cut the potatoes into thin slices three-quarters of the way through, leaving a thin uncut base so that they appear to be in a fan shape (see photograph page 109).
Melt half the butter in an ovenproof dish and place the potatoes in this. Sprinkle with salt and dot with the remaining butter. Bake in a hot oven for about 1 hour, depending on the size of the potatoes, basting occasionally. After 30 minutes, sprinkle with the grated cheese (if Parmesan is not available, choose a hard, slightly stale Cheddar) and breadcrumbs but do not baste any more. Potatoes cooked in this way are a delicious accompaniment to meat dishes.

Glazed potatoes

GLAZED POTATOES

D. BRUNEDE KARTOFLER
N. GLASERTE POTETER
S. GLASERAD POTATIS

Serve these potatoes with pork or beef dishes, or with chicken, roast duck, goose or game. In Scandinavia, plain boiled potatoes are frequently served together with glazed potatoes, at the same meal. Choose fairly small, even-sized ones for this recipe. New potatoes are the best but canned potatoes can also be used.

Preparation time 15 minutes
Cooking time 40 minutes
To serve 4

You will need

1½ lb. potatoes
water
salt

FOR GLAZING
3 tablespoons sugar
1½ oz. butter

Boil the potatoes in salted water until just tender, peel and leave them to cool. When cold, place in a colander and rinse under cold water; leave to drain. Melt the sugar in a frying pan and stir with a palette knife, until the sugar is beginning to turn brown. Do not let it burn. Remove the frying pan from the heat and add the butter, stir until it melts, then add the drained, but still moist, potatoes. Toss until the potatoes are evenly glazed and golden brown. Place the frying pan over gentle heat and cook until heated through. Serve at once (see photograph on book jacket).

HOT POTATO SALAD

D. VARM KARTOFFELSALAT

Choose small, firm potatoes for this dish, preferably new ones, cooked in their jackets. In Denmark, this recipe, served with Frankfurters, is very highly favoured.

Preparation time 15 minutes
Cooking time 40 minutes
To serve 4

You will need

1 oz. butter
2 medium-sized onions, sliced
4 tablespoons stock or water
4 tablespoons wine vinegar
½ teaspoon salt
pinch ground black pepper
sugar to taste (approximately 1 tablespoon)
1½ lb. cold, boiled potatoes, peeled and sliced

Melt the butter over low heat and add the onions. Cover the saucepan with a lid and gently fry the onions until they are transparent. Do not brown them. Add the stock and vinegar, season with salt, pepper and sugar and cook until the onions are tender. The hot dressing should be sweet-sour, so add more sugar if needed. Finally, add the potatoes and simmer over low heat until the potato salad is hot. Serve with hot frankfurter sausages and mustard.

CREAMED CURLY KALE

D. GRØNLANGKÅL
N. STUET GRÖNNKÅL
S. STUVAD GRÖNKÅL

Preparation time 20 minutes
Cooking time 20 minutes
To serve 4

You will need

2 lb. curly kale
water
salt

Cook the curly kale in boiling salted water for about 15 minutes. Drain, but retain the water and use this for the sauce. Prepare as for creamed spinach above, but use half milk and half vegetable water for the sauce.

RED CABBAGE

D. RØDKÅL
N. RÖDKÅL
S. RÖDKÅL

This is not only one of the most popular winter vegetables in Scandinavia, but is the one which is usually served at Christmas time. It goes particularly well with roast duck, goose or game, and also with pork dishes and sausages.

Preparation time 25 minutes
Cooking time approximately 2 hours
To serve 4—6

You will need

1 medium-sized red cabbage (approximately 2—3 lb.)
2 medium-sized cooking apples
1 oz. butter
6—8 tablespoons wine vinegar
6—8 tablespoons water
salt
pepper
4 tablespoons redcurrant jelly
sugar to taste (approximately 1—2 tablespoons)

Remove and discard the outer coarse leaves of the cabbage, cut it in half, remove the stalk and shred the cabbage very finely. Peel, core and grate the apples. Melt the butter in a large saucepan over low heat, add the cabbage and apples and toss for 5 minutes, taking care not to scorch. Add the vinegar, water, salt and pepper to taste, cover with a lid and cook over low heat, until cabbage is tender. Add redcurrant jelly and sugar to taste. The cabbage should be sweet-sour. Bring to the boil again and serve (see photograph on book jacket).
Red cabbage actually improves, if kept for a day before serving; just reheat it slowly, stirring from time to time. This dish is delicious eaten cold as a garnish for open sandwiches.
Note
The colour of the cooked cabbage may be improved by adding a little juice from pickled beetroots (see page 32).

VARIATION
Some caraway seed may be added to the dish whilst it is cooking.

Swedish baked potatoes

CREAMED SPINACH

D. STUVET SPINAT
N. STUET SPINAT
S. STUVAD SPENAT

Preparation time 20 minutes
Cooking time 5—8 minutes
To serve 4—6

You will need

1½ lb. fresh spinach *or*
  9 oz. packet frozen spinach
pinch of salt
¾ oz. butter
2 tablespoons plain flour
approximately ½ pint (U.S. 1¼ cups) milk
pinch pepper
grated nutmeg (optional)
pinch sugar

Clean and rinse the fresh spinach. Cook it with salt in a heavy saucepan covered with a lid for about 5 minutes, over very gentle heat. Drain the liquid from the spinach and chop the cooked leaves coarsely. Melt the butter in a saucepan and add the flour; gradually stir in the milk and cook the sauce for 3—5 minutes. Add the cooked spinach and reheat it. Add seasonings and serve the creamed spinach with egg dishes, meat or ham.

VARIATION

The spinach may be cooked for 3—4 minutes in the same way as above; add a lump of butter, a pinch of sugar and just before serving stir in a little double cream.

BOILED CELERIAC

D. KOGT SELLERI
N. KOKT SELLERIROT
S. KOKT ROTSELLERI

Preparation time 10 minutes
Cooking time   10—20 minutes

You will need

4—6 oz. celeriac, per person
water
2 teaspoons salt to each quart of water

Peel and rinse celeriac. Cut it into ½-inch thick slices. Put the sliced celeriac into boiling salted water and boil until just tender. Drain the slices and serve with creamed mushrooms (see this page), creamed sweetbreads or creamed shellfish piled on top (see pages 94 and 77).

VARIATION

The boiled celeriac slices may be dipped in beaten egg and dry brown breadcrumbs and then fried in butter on both sides; until golden brown. Serve hot with similar fillings to those suggested above.

GLAZED ONIONS

D. GLASEREDE LØG
N. GLASERT SMÅLÖK
S. GLASERAD LÖK

Preparation time 20 minutes
Cooking time   35 minutes
To serve   4—6

You will need

1½ lb. shallots
2 tablespoons sugar
1 oz. butter
stock or water

Pour boiling water over the shallots, then strain and peel them. Melt the sugar in a frying pan and when it begins to turn brown, add the butter. Stir, and toss in the onions, cook these in the caramel mixture over low to medium heat until evenly brown. Pour over sufficient stock or water to cover the onions and cook until they are tender. This will be about 20—30 minutes, depending on their size. Do not over-cook otherwise they will not retain their shape.
Serve with roast beef (see photograph page 98) or any other kind of roast meat. These are excellent for the smörgåsbord, either hot or cold.
Note
Small young carrots may be glazed and served in the same way.

CREAMED MUSHROOMS

D. CHAMPIGNONSTUVNING
N. SOPPSTUING
S. SVAMPSTUVNING

Mushrooms are used extensively in Scandinavian cooking: in salads, soups, casseroles and gravies. In salads they may be used either raw or cooked. The most common type is the *Champignon* which is similar to the English variety, but has a stronger flavour. *Chanterelles* is another favourite variety, found in the pine forests, particularly in Sweden. It obviously requires expert knowledge to distinguish between the edible fungi and the poisonous ones, but Scandinavians pride themselves on this knowledge and it is a favourite pastime to go on picnics to pick wild mushrooms. Fresh mushrooms should not be peeled or washed, but should simply have the hard ends of the stalks removed. The caps may be cleaned by rubbing with coarse salt and then wiping with a clean cloth.

Preparation time 15 minutes
Cooking time   10 minutes
To serve   4

You will need

1 lb. mushrooms, cleaned and sliced
2 oz. butter
salt
lemon juice to taste
generous ½ pint (U.S. 1¼ cups) double cream

Sauté the mushrooms in the butter for a few minutes. Add the salt and lemon juice and finally stir in the cream; cook for 3—5 minutes. Serve hot as a filling in an omelette, in pastry shells (see page 144) or on buttered toast.

CHEESE

Scandinavians are great cheese eaters, but cooked cheese is not on the whole a typical feature of their diet: recipes for cheese soufflés and cheese-flavoured biscuits follow, broadly speaking, those internationally known. Cheese may be served for breakfast, lunch or dinner. The different varieties appear on smørrebrød and a cheese tray is of course a standard feature of the smörgåsbord. For dinner, cheese is always served after the main course and before the dessert, as in France. This is surely a better idea than serving it at the end of the meal—especially if it is accompanied by red wine: you may then finish your wine before going on to the sweet.

A Scandinavian cheese tray is always arranged with great attention to detail. Fruit such as grapes, apples and nuts, as well as celery and radishes, form part of the arrangement, along with a variety of different types of bread and biscuits. The main difference between the Scandinavian and English ways of eating cheese reflects the smooth texture of most Scandinavian cheeses: they are cut into thin slices for layering on bread or biscuits, instead of being eaten in chunks.

Danish cheeses such as Danish Blue, Mycella, which is richer and creamier, Samsö, Danbo, Elbo, Fynbo, Esrom, and Havarti, are all exported and at least some of them are therefore familiar to many people; excellent Danish equivalents of Brie and Camembert are also produced and some very interesting smoked cream cheeses with caraway seeds are to be found. Sweden also has some caraway-flavoured cheeses, but the most common Swedish cheese varieties are Herrgårdsost and Svecia. Norway produces the famous nut-brown goat cheese but also has another speciality—the pungent Gammelost from Hardanger.

A selection of Danish cheeses: Havarti; Danbo with caraway seeds; Mycella; Esrom; Samsoe and Danish Blue

Cream cones served in sugar

DESSERTS

Everyday desserts consist simply of fruit in season, fresh or stewed, thickened with a little potato flour or cornflour and served with cream or custard. The latter is always a home-made concoction of eggs, cream or milk and vanilla. Cooked dried fruit such as apricots and prunes are also very popular, and neither is the latter considered a punishment! Sweet soups are made from apples, soft, red berries, or fresh rose hips, cooked, puréed and served hot or cold with cream, croûtons or spiced flour dumplings. Yoghurt, sour milk and pancakes of various sorts are all part of the daily fare according to season. Party desserts, on the other hand, are luscious creations of egg, cream, almonds, chocolate or fruit and are usually notable for their decorative appeal as well. Many of the cream layer cakes in the baking section also fall into the category of desserts. The ample use of rum in many puddings and cakes in the Danish cuisine presumably stems from the days when the Danes had colonies in the West Indies. Fruit syrups, preferably made from bottled morello cherries, go particularly well with many of these puddings. The contrasting sensation of a hot cherry sauce with a cold rum pudding is an exciting one, as is the combination of ice-cold whipped cream with hot puddings such as chocolate soufflé.

RED FRUIT PUDDING

D. RØDGRØD MED FLØDE
N. SAFTGRØT or FRUKTGRØT
S. SAFTKRÄM

This is probably the most famous and popular of all Scandinavian puddings. It can be made with redcurrants, blackcurrants or raspberries, but it is better to mix two or all three varieties together. The pudding is thickened with potato flour or cornflour, but it should not be stiff like a gelatine mixture. If you use potato flour, take care not to let the pudding boil, as this gives it a glutinous consistency. Fresh fruit, according to season, gives the best results, but canned or frozen fruit can be used, though the latter is not quite as satisfactory.

Preparation time 10 minutes
Cooking time   10 minutes
To serve   4—6

You will need

12 oz. redcurrants
12 oz. blackcurrants or raspberries
1½ pints (U.S. 3¾ cups) water
12 oz. sugar
2—3 level tablespoons cornflour
cold water
1½ oz. almonds, blanched and slivered
cream

Wash the fruit and place it in a saucepan with water. Simmer until tender and rub through a sieve. Pour fruit juice back into the saucepan and bring to the boil. Add the sugar and the cornflour, stirred to a thin paste with a little cold water. Boil for 2—3 minutes. When cool, pour into a glass serving dish, sprinkle a little sugar on top to prevent skin forming, sprinkle almonds over the top and leave to cool down completely, before serving with more sugar and chilled thick or thin cream served separately.

FRUIT-FILLED MELON

D. FYLDT MELON
N. FYLT MELON
S. FYLLD MELON

Melon is served as a sweet in Scandinavia rather than as a starter.

Preparation time 20 minutes
To serve 6

You will need

1 cantaloupe melon
sugar
1½—2 lb. wild or cultivated strawberries,
 raspberries, redcurrants or blackberries

Wash the melon and dry it. Cut off a lid or divide it into halves. It may be advisable to cut a thin slice from the base of the melon so that it will stand up. Remove the melon seeds and most of the flesh, using a spoon. Cut the flesh into cubes. Clean and rinse the fruit and put layers of fruit, melon cubes and sugar back into the hollowed-out melon. Chill and serve garnished with vine leaves.

DANISH STRAWBERRY MEDALLIONS

D. JORDBÆR MEDALJER

Fresh or frozen strawberries can be used for this recipe. If frozen ones are used, drain off some of the juice before mixing with the cream or mixture will become too runny.

Preparation time 10 minutes
Cooking time 8 minutes
Oven temperature 425°F. Gas Mark 7

You will need

9 oz. plain flour
7 oz. butter
2½ oz. icing sugar, sifted
2 egg yolks
8 oz. strawberries, cleaned and hulled
2 level tablespoons castor sugar
vanilla sugar to taste
½ pint (U.S. 1¼ cups) double cream, stiffly
 whipped

FOR DECORATION
icing sugar
halved strawberries

Sift the flour and rub in the butter with finger-tips; add the icing sugar and egg yolks and knead lightly. Put the pastry aside in a cool place until it is slightly firmer. Roll out the pastry ¼-inch thick on a floured board and cut into round biscuits, using a 2½-inch cutter or a glass. Bake for approximately 8 minutes in a very hot oven. Cool on a wire tray. Just before serving, mash the strawberries lightly with a fork and mix in the sugar and vanilla sugar. Fold the strawberries in to the whipped cream. Sandwich the biscuits together with the strawberry cream filling, dust the top of the biscuits with icing sugar and place a halved strawberry on top of each.

DANISH PRINCESS PUDDING

D. PRINSESSEBUDDING

Preparation time 15 minutes
Cooking time 1½—2 hours
To serve 4—6

You will need

4 oz. butter
4 oz. plain flour, sifted
12 fl. oz. (U.S. 1½ cups) single cream *or*
 scalded milk
vanilla sugar to taste
6 egg yolks
5 level dessertspoons sugar
6 egg whites, stiffly beaten
toasted brown breadcrumbs

Melt the butter in a saucepan and add the flour. Do not let it brown. Gradually stir in the scalded milk or cream, while it is still hot. Stir all the time until the mixture is smooth. Remove the saucepan from heat and add the vanilla sugar. Stir in the egg yolks, one at a time, beating vigorously after the addition of each yolk. Add the sugar and stir well. Finally, fold in the beaten egg whites.
Sprinkle a well-greased, 3-pint mould with dry breadcrumbs and pour in the batter. Sprinkle more breadcrumbs on top and cover with aluminium foil. Secure with string and lower the mould into a large saucepan with simmering water coming two-thirds of the way up the sides of the mould. Cover the saucepan with a lid and simmer the pudding over very low heat for 1½—2 hours. Replenish the sauce-pan with warm water as needed—do not allow to boil, or the pudding will have holes like a sponge. When cooked, turn out carefully on to a serving dish and serve at once with hot Fruit Juice sauce (see page 126).

Marzipan cakes; Othello layer cake; rum pudding and white wine jelly

Danish birthday pretzel

A selection of Danish pastries: windmills; snails; a plait and a butter cake

Swedish cream waffles

VEILED COUNTRY LASS

D. BONDEPIGE MED SLØR

I confess that I really have no idea how this dish got its fascinating name—perhaps because its solid, homely base is topped with a more frivolous layer of whipped cream.

Preparation time 30 minutes
Cooking time 15 minutes
To serve 4

You will need

2 lb. cooking apples
3 oz. granulated sugar
2 oz. butter
8 oz. dark Danish rye bread, grated
¼ pint (U.S. ⅔ cup) double cream, whipped
2 oz. dark chocolate, grated

Peel, core and slice the apples and cook them in a covered, heavy-based saucepan, without any water over gentle heat. When the apples are tender, stir 2 oz. of the sugar into them, then leave to cool. Melt the butter in a frying pan and fry the grated rye bread, mixed with the sugar, until crisp. When the apples are cold, place alternate layers of these and the breadcrumbs in a glass dish, finishing with a layer of breadcrumbs. Decorate with whipped cream and sprinkle grated chocolate on top.

CHOCOLATE SOUFFLÉ

D. CHOKOLADE SOUFFLÉ

This old Danish family recipe is delicious because of the piquant flavour of the honey blending with the chocolate. Serve it straight from the oven.

Preparation time 10 minutes
Cooking time 25 minutes
Oven temperature 375°F. Gas Mark 5
To serve 4

You will need

1 tablespoon thick honey
6 large egg yolks
2 level tablespoons granulated sugar
7 oz. dark cooking chocolate
1 tablespoon strong coffee
1 oz. blanched slivered almonds (optional)
6 large egg whites, stiffly beaten
chilled whipped cream

Spread the honey thinly over the bottom of a 3-pint soufflé dish. Whisk the egg yolks with the sugar until frothy. Meanwhile, melt the chocolate with the coffee over low heat—do not let it boil. Add the almonds to the egg yolks and gradually stir in the warm, melted chocolate. Cool completely, before folding in the stiffly beaten egg whites. Pour into the greased soufflé dish and cook for 25 minutes in the hottest part of the oven. Serve at once with chilled whipped cream served separately.

DANISH PRUNE SOUFFLÉ

D. SVESKE SOUFFLÉ

Preparation time 15 minutes
Cooking time 25—30 minutes
Oven temperature 475°F. Gas Mark 7
To serve 6

You will need

1 lb. prunes
water
sugar to taste
approximately 1 oz. almonds, blanched and slivered
¼ pint (U.S. ⅔ cup) soured cream or fresh cream and juice and grated rind of ½ lemon
4 medium-thick slices of stale white bread, with crusts removed
4 egg yolks
2 oz. sugar
4 egg whites, stiffly beaten
whipped cream

FOR DECORATION
a few whole almonds, blanched

Rinse the prunes, leave them to soak in hot water for several hours, and then cook them over a low heat for 15 minutes, with sugar to taste. Drain, remove the stones and replace each stone with a blanched almond. Place the prunes in a well-greased 3-pint soufflé dish. Pour the cream into a mixing bowl, crumble the bread into the cream, and add the almonds. Beat the egg yolks with the sugar until frothy; add to the cream and bread mixture and stir. Fold in the beaten egg whites and pour the mixture on top of the prunes. Bake in a hot to very hot oven. Serve hot with whipped cream served separately.

VARIATION
Fresh plums may be used for this recipe instead of prunes. Remove the stones and replace them with almonds. Sprinkle liberally with sugar.

APPLE AND ALMOND PUDDING

D. ÆBLE OG MANDEL DESSERT

Preparation time 35 minutes
Cooking time 35 minutes
Oven temperature 375°F. Gas Mark 5
To serve 4

You will need

1½ lb. cooking apples, cored, peeled and
    sliced
1 oz. butter
1 small glass brandy (optional)
sugar to taste
4 egg yolks
2 oz. sugar
½ oz. plain flour
¼ pint double cream
2 oz. ground almonds

Cook the apples with the butter in a heavy-based
saucepan, until tender. Add the brandy and stir in
the sugar. Pour the stewed apples into a 2-pint
soufflé dish.
Whisk the egg yolks and sugar until foaming white.
Add the flour, cream and ground almonds. Stir, and
pour the mixture over the stewed apples. Cook in a
fairly hot oven for 35 minutes. Serve the pudding hot
with chilled whipped cream.

BAKED APPLES WITH ALMOND FILLING

D. BAGTE FYLDTE ÆBLER
N. STEKTE FYLTE EPLER
S. STEKTA FYLLDA ÄPPLEN

Preparation time 25 minutes
Cooking time 30—40 minutes
Oven temperature 355°F. Gas Mark 4

You will need

4 large cooking apples
1—2 tablespoons melted butter
4—5 tablespoons browned breadcrumbs
almond paste (see page 131)

Rinse and dry the apples, then peel and core them.
Brush with melted butter and roll them in browned
breadcrumbs. Place the apples in a buttered, ovenproof dish and fill the centres with the almond paste.
Pour the remaining butter over them and bake in a
moderate oven for 30—40 minutes until soft. Serve
hot with thick whipped cream or with vanilla
cream (see page 122).

APPLE CAKE

D. ÆBLEKAGE
N. EPLEKAKE
S. ÄPPELKAKA

This is one of the most common and popular desserts
in Scandinavia. There are any number of variations.
The crumbs used may be toasted brown breadcrumbs, rusks, macaroons or a combination of all
three. The recipe is similar to the English Apple
Charlotte. In Denmark, the applecake is usually
served decorated with whipped cream and redcurrant or apple jelly; in Norway, the whipped
cream is often used both as a filling between the
layers and as decoration on top, whilst in Sweden
the applecake is usually baked and served cold with
a vanilla sauce.

Preparation time 15 minutes
Cooking time 15 minutes
To serve 4

You will need

2 lb. cooking apples
3 tablespoons water
sugar to taste
2 oz. butter
4½ oz. toasted brown breadcrumbs
2 oz. granulated sugar

Peel and core the apples, slice them and cook with
water, over very low heat until soft enough to purée.
Rub through a sieve, add sugar to taste and leave to
cool. Melt the butter in a frying pan, add breadcrumbs and sugar and cook over medium heat,
stirring all the time, until the breadcrumbs begin
to turn brown. Remove the pan from heat, but keep
stirring until the breadcrumbs cool down. When
they are cold, place alternate layers of breadcrumbs and apple purée in a serving dish, beginning
and finishing with breadcrumbs. Chill, decorate
with whipped cream and serve. (See photograph
page 121).
Note
Apple cake is best when eaten soon after it has been
made. If made in advance, the crumbs become
soggy.

SWEDISH APPLE CAKE WITH VANILLA SAUCE

S. ÄPPELKAKA MED VANILJSÅS

Use the same ingredients as for Apple cake on page 120 and add 1 oz. blanched almonds.

Oven temperature 375°F. Gas Mark 5
To serve   4

Make layers with breadcrumbs and apple purée in a well buttered, baking dish, beginning and ending with breadcrumbs. Dot with a little butter and bake for 30 minutes in a moderate oven. Leave to cool before turning out of the mould. Decorate with blanched almonds and serve with vanilla sauce (see below).

VANILLA SAUCE

D. VANILLE CREMESAUCE
N. VANILJESAUS
S. VANILJSÅS

This rich sweet vanilla sauce, or custard, is usually served with the baked Swedish Apple cake. It is also good with the Wine Jelly as an alternative to Vanilla Cream.

Preparation time 10 minutes
Cooking time   10 minutes
To serve   4

You will need

scant ½ pint (U.S. I cup) single cream
¼—½ vanilla pod, split
3 egg yolks
2 tablespoons granulated sugar
¼ pint (U.S. ⅔ cup) double cream, whipped
   (a little top of milk may be added, if cream
   is very thick)

Boil the single cream and the split vanilla pod in a saucepan with a heavy base; remove the saucepan from the heat, cover it with a lid and leave it to stand for 10 minutes. Remove the vanilla pod, dry and store it in sugar for further use. Beat the egg yolks with the sugar in the top of a double boiler. Reheat the cream and when it boils add it to the egg mixture, stirring constantly until thick. Do not let it boil. Remove from heat, and when the custard is completely cold, carefully fold in the whipped cream.

Apple cake

Swedish apple cake

MOLEHILLS

D. MULDVARPESKUD

This is a Danish sweet which delights children and appeals to adults as well.

Preparation time 35 minutes
Cooking time 20 minutes
To serve 4—6

You will need

9 oz. prunes
approximately 2 pints water
3—4 oz. sugar
juice of half lemon
blanched almonds (optional)
1 portion Vanilla Cream (see below)
2 oz. dark Danish rye bread, grated
2 oz. dark cooking chocolate, grated

Rinse the prunes and soak them overnight in the cold water. Cook them in the same water until they are tender, about 15 minutes. Add the sugar and lemon juice, stir and simmer for a few more minutes. Drain the prunes and remove the stones. Replace each stone with a blanched almond if liked, then heap the stuffed prunes on to a serving dish and leave to chill. Just before serving, pour the Vanilla Cream over the prunes and decorate with grated rye bread and chocolate.

VANILLA CREAM

D. RAA CREME

Preparation time 8 minutes
To serve 4

You will need

2 egg yolks
$\frac{3}{4}$ oz. castor sugar
1 teaspoon vanilla sugar
8 fl. oz. (U.S. 1 cup) double cream, chilled
   and whipped

Stir the egg yolks with the sugar and vanilla sugar until thick and frothy.
Just before serving, carefully fold in the whipped cream. Serve with Wine Jelly (see page 123).

CONES WITH WHIPPED CREAM 1.

D. KRÆMMERHUSE MED FLØDESKUM
N. FYLTE KRUMKAKER
S. STRUTAR MED FYLLNING

These cones can be stored in air-tight tins for several weeks. The recipe is a useful one for finishing up surplus egg whites.

Preparation time 15 minutes
Cooking time 5—6 minutes
Oven temperature 400°F. Gas Mark 6
Makes approximately 25

You will need

$4\frac{1}{2}$ oz. butter
$4\frac{1}{2}$ oz. sugar
$4\frac{1}{2}$ oz. plain flour, sifted
4 large egg whites, stiffly beaten
whipped cream
strawberry jam

Cream the butter and sugar, add the sifted flour and fold in the beaten egg whites. Stir the mixture gently.
Heavily grease a baking sheet and drop teaspoons of the batter, at least 2 inches apart, on to it. Using a palette knife, dipped in cold water, shape the dough into thin circles and bake 2—3 at a time for approximately 5—6 minutes, in a moderately hot to hot oven. The biscuits are ready when they begin to turn brown around the edges. Loosen carefully with a palette knife and roll into cone shapes whilst still hot. Work quickly; place the cones in a bottle neck or a glass to cool, stacking them inside one another to keep them in shape. Immediately before serving, fill the cones with whipped cream and place a little strawberry jam on top. To serve, stand the cones in sugar in a deep dish (see photograph page 112).

CONES WITH WHIPPED CREAM 2.

D. KRÆMMERHUSE MED FLØDESKUM
N. FYLTE KRUMKAKER
S. STRUTAR MED FYLLNING

Preparation time 15 minutes
Cooking time 5—6 minutes
Oven temperature 400°F. Gas Mark 6
Makes approximately 25

You will need

3 medium-sized eggs
5 oz. sugar
3 tablespoons water
3½ oz. plain, sifted flour

Beat the whole eggs with the sugar and water, add the sifted flour and proceed with the baking of cones as previous recipe.

VARIATION

As an alternative to whipped cream, fill the cones with a purée of cooked fruit, mixed with a stiffly beaten egg white.

ICE CREAM

D. PARFAIT
N. PARFAIT
S. GLASS

Preparation time 10—15 minutes
To serve 6

You will need

5 egg yolks
2½ oz. sugar
½ vanilla pod
1 pint (U.S. 2½ cups) double cream, whipped

Whisk the egg yolks and sugar to a thick foam. Split the vanilla pod and scrape the seeds into the egg mixture. Finally, whip the cream and fold this into the egg mixture; pour the mixture into the ice-tray of the refrigerator or into a mould and freeze in the refrigerator or freezer, without stirring, for 4—5 hours. Turn the ice cream out on to a serving dish and decorate as a mould or serve sliced and decorate the slices with fruit or grated chocolate.

VARIATIONS

The following ingredients may be added to the whipped cream before this is folded into the egg mixture:
1. Coffee: approximately 3—4 oz. very strong black coffee.
2. Chocolate: approximately 7 oz. grated dark chocolate.
3. Caramel: approximately 5—6 oz. sugar.
4. Macaroons: approximately 7 oz. crushed macaroons.
5. Fruit juice or fresh or canned fruit.

Shaping cream cones

RED WINE JELLY

D. RØDVINSGELÉ

Sweet artificially flavoured jellies are not, I am glad to say, used in Scandinavian cooking. In Denmark, jelly is made either with pure fruit juice or, as in the following two sophisticated recipes, with wine—thus catering for the adult taste rather than the child's They are easy to make and look splendid for a party, and they go especially well as a sweet when a game course has been served as the main part of the meal. If you have served red wine with the main course, choose white wine jelly to follow, in preference to red, and vice versa.

Preparation time 10 minutes
Cooking time 5 minutes
To serve 6—8

You will need

½ pint water
2—3 oz. sugar
16 thin leaves of gelatine *or*
    8 level teaspoons powdered gelatine
1 pint (U.S. 2½ cups) red wine
½ pint (U.S. 1¼ cups) red fruit juice
    (raspberry, cherry or any other soft fruit)

Boil the water and sugar. Melt the gelatine according to instructions for Scandinavian Rice Pudding on page 125 and add it to the water and sugar. Stir in the red wine and fruit juice. Pour the red wine mixture into a wetted 3-pint (U.S. 7½ cups) mould, and leave it in a cold place until set.
Turn the jelly out on to a serving dish and serve with either Vanilla Sauce or Vanilla Cream (see pages 121 and 122).

123

Caramel custard with caramel-flavoured whipped cream

CARAMEL CUSTARD

D. KARAMELRAND
N. KARAMELLPUDDING
S. BRYLÉPUDDING

In Norway and Sweden, this pudding is served with blanched almonds arranged in a pattern on top with the caramel sauce served separately. In Denmark the pudding is served with the centre of the dish filled up with the caramel sauce blended with stiffly whipped cream, as shown in the photograph.

Preparation time 20 minutes
Cooking time 30—35 minutes
Oven temperature 350°F. Gas Mark 4
To serve 4—6

You will need

7 oz. granulated sugar
generous ¼ pint (U.S. ¾ cup) boiling water
1 pint (U.S. 2½ cups) single cream
½ vanilla pod
5 large eggs
1 oz. sugar
½ oz. blanched almonds *or*
generous ¼ pint (U.S. ¾ cup) double cream, whipped

Melt the sugar in a heavy frying pan and stir until it is brown, but not burnt. Pour two-thirds of this caramel into a warm 2½-pint (U.S. 6¼ cups) ring mould, and coat the bottom and sides with it. Add the boiling water to the remaining caramel in the frying pan and cook over low heat until the caramel sauce is smooth.
Bring the cream to the boil with the vanilla pod. Meanwhile, lightly beat the eggs and sugar in a basin. Remove the vanilla pod and pour the boiling cream onto the eggs and sugar. Stir gently. Pour the custard through a fine sieve into the caramel-coated mould or ring; place this on a rack in a baking pan with warm water to reach two-thirds of the way up the mould. Bake in a moderate oven for 40—45 minutes, until the custard is set. Check to see if the custard is cooked by plunging a knife into it and seeing if it comes out clean. Make sure that the water in the pan does not boil, or the custard will be full of holes.
Leave the custard to cool down completely before turning it out of the mould onto a serving dish.

WHITE WINE JELLY

D. HVIDVINSGELÉ

Preparation time 30 minutes
Cooking time 5 minutes
To serve 6—8

You will need

8 fl. oz. (U.S. 1 cup) water
5 oz. sugar
16 leaves gelatine *or*
  8 level teaspoons powdered gelatine
1 pint white wine
6 fl. oz. (U.S. ¾ cup) sweet sherry
1—1½ lb. white grapes

Boil the water and sugar. Melt the gelatine (see Scandinavian Rice Pudding, page 125) and add it to the water and sugar. Stir in the white wine and the sherry.
Halve the grapes and remove the pips. Line a wetted ring-shaped 3-pint (U.S. 7½ cups) mould with some of the grapes and pour over a little of the white wine mixture; leave to set before repeating the process. Continue until the mould is full and leave it in a cold place to set. Turn the jelly out on to a serving dish (see photograph page 115) and serve with either Vanilla Sauce or Vanilla Cream (see pages 121 and 122).

CHRISTMAS RICE PORRIDGE

D. RISENGRØD
N. RISGRYNSGRÖT
S. RISGRYNSGRÖT

Rice porridge is part of the traditional Christmas Eve dinner in all three Scandinavian countries, but in Denmark porridge is served as a first course before the roast duck, goose or pork. No doubt the idea was originally to take the edge off your appetite before going onto the main course. Applecake follows the main course, as a pudding. The more sophisticated version of rice pudding, ris à l'amande, often replaces applecake, in which case the rice porridge is obviously also omitted.

Traditionally, on Christmas Eve a whole almond is placed in the rice porridge or pudding and the lucky finder is rewarded with a present—often in the shape of a delectable prize made out of marzipan. Rice porridge or puddings are cooked on top of the stove and not in the oven as in English cooking. The renowned brown skin on rice pudding is unfamiliar to Scandinavians and would probably be frowned upon!

Preparation time 8 minutes
Cooking time 1 hour
To serve 4

You will need

2 pints (U.S. 5 cups) milk
4½ oz. short grained rice
½ teaspoon salt
sugar
ground cinnamon

Bring the milk to the boil in a heavy saucepan. Rinse the rice in cold water. Add the rice to the boiling milk while stirring. Lower the heat, cover with a lid, and gently cook the rice for about 1 hour. Add the salt and stir. Serve the hot porridge with a lump of cold butter placed in the centre of each portion and sprinkle with sugar and ground cinnamon.

Note
Any rice porridge which is left over may be used for making tarts with rice filling (see page 138).

SCANDINAVIAN RICE PUDDING

D. RIS À L'AMANDE
N. RIS À LA MALTA or RISKREM
S. RIS À LA MALTA

In many Danish homes this sophisticated rice pudding has replaced the traditional rice porridge served on Christmas Eve. The recipe obviously stems from the French cuisine as its name suggests, though it has undergone some changes on its route northwards.

Preparation time 10 minutes
Cooking time 20 minutes
To serve 4

You will need

scant ¾ pint (U.S. 1¾ cups) milk
1½ oz. short grained rice
½ vanilla pod *or*
    vanilla sugar to taste
1 oz. almonds, blanched and coarsely
    chopped
3 thin leaves gelatine *or*
    1—2 teaspoons powdered gelatine, dissolved in 1 tablespoon water
scant ½ pint (U.S. 1 cup) double cream,
    stiffly whipped

Note
If leaf gelatine is used, soak the leaves for 10 minutes, drain, squeeze out the surplus water and melt in a double saucepan over low heat. If using powdered gelatine, mix it with 1 tablespoon of cold water and allow to set. Dissolve the cake of gelatine in a small saucepan, over very gentle heat. Do not allow it to boil.
Rinse a saucepan with cold water, pour in the milk and bring to the boil. Wash the rice and add to the boiling milk together with the vanilla pod. (If vanilla sugar is used, add when rice is cooked). Stir constantly for the first 5 minutes, then reduce the heat and continue to cook for a further 15 minutes. When cooked, remove the vanilla pod, add the sugar and leave the rice to cool down. Stir in the almonds and, meanwhile, prepare the gelatine. Add the melted gelatine to the cold rice pudding and finally fold in the whipped cream. Chill the pudding and serve it with hot Fruit Juice sauce (see page 126).

NORWEGIAN RICE PUDDING

N. RIS À LA MALTA or RISKREM

Preparation time 10 minutes
Cooking time 20 minutes
To serve 4

You will need

3 oz. short-grained rice
2 pints (U.S. 5 cups) water
2 tablespoons granulated sugar
1 tablespoon grated lemon peel
generous ½ pint (U.S. 1½ cups) double cream
jam or jelly

Boil the water and add the washed rice. Leave it to boil for 20 minutes. Drain and rinse, in a sieve, under cold water and leave to drain thoroughly. Meanwhile, add the sugar and lemon peel to the cream and whip until thick. Add the rice to the cream and pour into a serving dish. Decorate with jam or jelly and serve chilled.

FRUIT JUICE SAUCE

D. SAFTSAUCE
N. SAFTSAUS
S. SAFTSÅS

Preparation time 5 minutes
Cooking time 5 minutes
To serve 4—6

You will need

10 oz. cooked or bottled Morello cherries *or*
   black cherries in heavy syrup or
   ½ pint (U.S. 1¼ cups) red fruit syrup
1 level tablespoon cornflour, stirred with a
   little cold water

Bring the bottled fruit and the syrup to boil. Add the cornflour, and simmer for 2—3 minutes. Serve hot with cold rum pudding, or Princess pudding (see below, and page 114).

DANISH RUM PUDDING

D. ROMBUDDING

This old Danish recipe may be a rather extravagant one, but it makes a delicious and elegant dessert for festive occasions.

Preparation time 20 minutes
Cooking time 5 minutes
To serve 6—8

You will need

10 thin leaves gelatine *or*
   6 teaspoons powdered gelatine
4 large egg yolks
5 oz. granulated sugar
3 tablespoons rum
1 pint (U.S. 2½ cups) single cream
½ vanilla pod
½ pint (U.S. 1¼ cups) double cream, whipped

Prepare gelatine as in recipe for Scandinavian Rice Pudding (see page 125). Beat the egg yolks with sugar and rum until thick and frothy. Meanwhile, bring the cream to the boil with the vanilla pod. Remove the saucepan from the heat and remove the vanilla pod; add the melted gelatine. Stir the single cream into the egg, sugar and rum mixture and leave to cool, stirring from time to time. When the rum custard is beginning to set, fold in the whipped cream. Pour into a mould and leave in the refrigerator to set for several hours or until the following day. Turn the mould out on to a serving dish and serve the pudding with hot Fruit Juice sauce (see recipe this page and photograph page 115).

SWEDISH CREAM WAFFLES

S. FRASVÅFFLOR

Preparation time 10—15 minutes
Cooking time 2—3 minutes each waffle
To serve 4—6

You will need

5½ oz. plain flour
6 tablespoons cold water
14 fl. oz. (U.S. 1¾ cups) double cream,
   whipped
2 oz. melted butter, cooled

Sift the flour into a basin and mix it with the cold water. Fold in the whipped cream and leave the batter to stand for 1 hour, then carefully stir in the cold, melted butter. Heat the waffle iron and brush it with butter. Pour in a few tablespoons of the batter and cook over medium heat for 3—4 minutes until the waffle is golden brown on both sides. Repeat this process until all the batter is used. Place the baked waffles on a wire tray to keep crisp. Serve immediately with sugar or jam and whipped cream. The waffles look particularly pretty when baked in an old-fashioned heart-shaped waffle iron (see photograph page 118).

DANISH DOUGHNUTS

D. ÆBLESKIVER

It is difficult to know how best to translate *Æbleskiver*. Although they are usually called Danish Doughnuts, they are not really doughnuts at all. They are cooked in a special pan called an *æbleskivepande*. This is a special pan which may be obtained in any of the big stores which stock Nacco products. These pans are also useful for cooking Danish rissoles (see page 92) and whole tomatoes. The Danish name literally means 'apple slices', and comes from the custom of placing a piece of apple in the centre of each Danish doughnut, but they are also very tasty without the apple, if dipped in icing sugar.

Preparation time 5 minutes
Cooking time 6—8 minutes each doughnut
To serve 4

You will need

4½ oz. plain flour
½ teaspoon baking powder
1 teaspoon ground cardamom *or*
　grated lemon rind
¼ pint milk
3 tablespoons beer
2 eggs, separated
2 oz. melted butter
1 tablespoon granulated sugar
¼ teaspoon salt
butter for frying
icing sugar

Sift the flour and baking powder and add the cardamom or lemon rind. Stir in the milk, beer, egg yolks and melted butter. Add the granulated sugar and salt and stir to a fairly thick, smooth batter. Beat the egg whites until stiff and fold them lightly into

Cooking Danish doughnuts

Turning Danish doughnuts

the batter. Pour a little butter for frying into each cup of the heated doughnut pan and then fill the cups two-thirds full with the batter. Cook over a medium to strong heat for about 3 minutes, until the doughnuts are set underneath. Turn them over with a metal knitting needle or skewer and finish cooking on the other side for 2—3 minutes, until they are golden all over. Serve hot with icing sugar.

VARIATION
A teapoon of jam or a thin slice of raw apple may be placed in the centre of each doughnut before turning it over.

Mazarins and medals on cake stand; custard cream tarts and almond mussels on wooden tray

BAKING

No Scandinavian cookery book would be complete without a recipe section on so-called 'Danish pastries' or *Wienerbröd*. It would, however, be wrong to suggest that the average Danish housewife very often goes to the trouble of making these herself; she is much more likely to buy her Danish pastries at one of the many '*Konditorier*' or pastry shops which visitors to Denmark find so tempting. Amongst the other attractions of these shops are the layer cakes, made from several thin layers of pastry or sponge, sandwiched together with rich creamy fillings and sumptuously decorated with more cream or thin icings, fruit, chocolate or marzipan—all guaranteed to add inches to your waist-line. Almonds are used extensively in baking, either whole or ground, their crowning glory being the Danish marzipan cakes. For festive occasions such as weddings, confirmations and christenings, these are built up out of a multitude of rings shaped into cornucopias or small towers and decorated with icing, like the photograph on page 115.

In spite of the temptations of the pastry shops, home baking is still very much alive in all Scandinavian countries, particularly at Christmas time. A multitude of traditional biscuits and gingerbreads are made, including gingerbread houses, decorated with icing for the benefit of the children. Coffee bread, a yeast mixture which is shaped into various loaves, twists, cakes and buns, is particularly popular in Norway and Sweden, where saffron-coloured coffee bread buns, or *Lussekatter*, are baked for 13th December when the Swedes celebrate the feast of Santa Lucia. Baking with yeast, whether for bread or cakes, is easy and very often quicker than making an elaborate cake. After all, you do not have to sit and watch the dough rise; you can get on with other things, and the preparation is very simple. Cakes made from choux or short pastry and mille feuilles with various fillings are very popular, and so are various soft cakes, such as sand cake, and others flavoured with cardamom, cinnamon or vanilla with the addition of peel, currants and raisins. The absence of heavy fruit cakes and of thick and elaborate icing also distinguishes Scandinavian baking.

MACAROON CAKE

D. MAKRONBUND

Preparation time 10 minutes
Cooking time 20—25 minutes
Oven temperature 335°F. Gas Mark 3

You will need

3½ oz. ground almonds
2½ oz. granulated sugar
1 level teaspoon baking powder
2 egg whites, beaten

Mix the ground almonds with the sugar and baking powder; add the egg whites and stir thoroughly until the mixture is thick and smooth. Spread into a 9—10 inch round sandwich tin, which has been lined with well-greased foil or rice paper. Bake in a very moderate oven for approximately 20—25 minutes. Because of the absence of flour this cake is very fragile and must be turned out carefully on to a wire rack and left to cool.

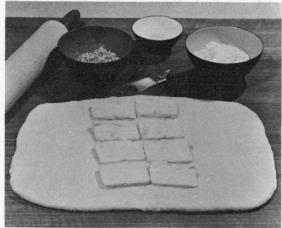
Placing the butter on Danish pastry

Folded Danish pastry dough

DANISH PASTRY

D. WIENERBRÖD

As you see from the Danish name above, Vienna is credited with being the place of origin for Danish pastries. The dough is a rich, puff pastry made with yeast and butter. It lends itself to a variety of different pastries. If you own a freezer, it is worth knowing that the pastries may be frozen either before or after baking.

The following points are important to remember:
1. Always prepare all fillings in advance as the dough should not be proved before rolling.
2. The butter used for rolling in, should be of the same consistency as the dough.
3. The pastries should always be baked in a very hot oven.

Preparation time 1—2 hours
Cooking time 12 minutes
Oven temperature 450°F. Gas Mark 8
Makes about 30 pastries

You will need

1 lb. plain flour
1 teaspoon salt
1 oz. sugar
1 teaspoon ground cardamom
2 oz. yeast
8 fl. oz. (U.S. 1 cup) cold milk *or*
    equal quantities of milk and water
1 egg
10 oz. butter

Sift the flour, salt, sugar and cardamom into a bowl. Cream the yeast with a little of the cold milk and add to the flour with the remainder of the milk and the beaten egg. Mix to a dough and work until smooth and shiny. Roll to a 14-inch square, about

½ inch thick, on a lightly floured board. Cut the butter into slices and place these side by side over the centre third of the dough (see photograph above) taking care that the butter does not cover the edges. Fold over a third of the dough from one end, to cover the butter, then fold over the remaining third (see photograph above). Seal the ends with a rolling pin and store in a cold place for 15 minutes. Roll the dough out to its former size, fold in the same way at right angles to the previous folds, and leave in a cold place for a further 15 minutes. Repeat this process once more. Place the dough in a floured plastic bag and allow it to rest for 15 minutes before using.

The shaped, filled pastries should be placed on ungreased baking sheets. Leave them to prove for 10-15 minutes in a warm place. (Do not prove in a place which is too warm, or the butter will run).

FILLING FOR DANISH PASTRIES

D. INDLÆG TIL WIENERBRØD

Preparation time 5 minutes

You will need

4½ oz. crushed macaroons *or*
    finely chopped blanched almonds
4½ oz. butter
4½ oz. castor sugar

Mix the macaroons or almonds with the butter and sugar and stir until smooth, but not too soft.

ALMOND PASTE

D. MANDELMASSE
N. MARSIPAN
S. MANDELMASSA

Preparation time 10 minutes

You will need

8 oz. almonds
8 oz. icing sugar
egg white

Blanch the almonds and grind them twice, the second time together with the sugar. Add egg white a little at a time and work the mixture vigorously, either on a pastry board or in a mortar with a pestle. The mixture should be firm and smooth when ready. The paste may be used for the filling of Swedish Lenten Buns, or covering cakes such as the Othello Layer Cake (see page 139).

BUTTER FILLING

You will need

4½ oz. unsalted butter
4 tablespoons icing sugar
3 tablespoons currants, washed and dried

Cream butter with the icing sugar and add the currants.

SPANDAU

D. SPANDAU

Preparation time 30 minutes
Cooking time 10—12 minutes
Oven temperature 450°F. Gas Mark 8
Makes 8

You will need

¼ quantity Danish pastry (see page 130)
approximately 3—4 oz. custard cream
  filling (see page 137)
1 tablespoon jam
water icing (see page 139)
beaten egg

Roll out the pastry into a 12-inch square. Cut into 16 squares. Put a blob of custard cream filling in the centre of each and spread some jam over the top. Fold over the four corners to meet in the middle and press them down. Leave the pastries on baking sheets to prove for 15 minutes. Brush with beaten egg and bake in a very hot oven for about 10—12 minutes. Leave the pastries to cool down and brush with water icing (see page 139).

COCK'S COMB

D. HANEKAM

Preparation time 30 minutes
Cooking time 10—12 minutes
Oven temperature 450°F. Gas Mark 8
Makes 8

You will need

¼ quantity Danish pastry (see page 130)
approximately 3 oz. apple purée *or*
  macaroon filling (see page 130)
beaten egg
½ oz. chopped almonds *or*
  sugar crystals

Roll out the pastry to a 12-inch square. Spread apple purée or macaroon filling down the centre. Fold the dough in half and seal the edges. Cut into 1½-inch wide pieces and make incisions ¾-inch apart in the cut edge of each piece. Bend each cock's comb so that it fans out (see photograph) and place on baking sheets to prove for 15 minutes. Brush with beaten egg and scatter with chopped almonds or sugar crystals. Bake in a very hot oven for 10—12 minutes.

Cock's combs and envelopes

Snails

DANISH BIRTHDAY PRETZEL

D. KRINGLE

Preparation time 30—45 minutes
Cooking time 20—25 minutes
Oven temperature 450—475°F. Gas Mark 7—8
To serve 8—10

You will need

2 oz. fresh yeast
2 oz. granulated sugar
1 lb. plain white flour
8 fl. oz. milk (U.S. 1 cup) milk
1 standard egg
7 oz. very cold butter
a little beaten egg
filling for Danish pastries (see page 130)
1 oz. almonds, blanched, peeled and coarsely
    chopped
1 tablespoon sugar crystals

Hot chocolate with whipped cream is a traditional birthday treat and is usually served with a Danish birthday pretzel.

Cream the yeast with the sugar in a basin. Sift the flour into a large mixing bowl. Whisk the milk and egg and add to the flour, together with the creamed yeast. Mix well. Leave the dough in a cold place for 1 hour. Roll out the dough to a rectangle, approximately 22 by 12 inches. Cut the cold butter into slices and place these, side by side, over the middle

Windmills

third of the dough, but not near the edges. Fold over one third of dough to cover the butter, then fold the remaining third over the top. Seal the ends with a rolling pin and store in a cold place for 15 minutes. Roll and fold the dough as for puff pastry (see page 134). After the last rolling and folding, the dough is ready for use. Roll out into a long strip, about 3-4 inches wide and $\frac{1}{8}$ inch thick. Spread the centre with the previously prepared filling (see page 130). Turn over the edges to cover the filling, form into a figure-of-eight pretzel shape, and place on a well-greased baking sheet. Leave in a warm, but not hot, place for a further 15 minutes. Brush with beaten egg and scatter chopped almonds and sugar crystals on top. Bake towards the top of a very hot oven for approximately 15—20 minutes (see photograph page 116).

SNAIL

D. SNEGL

Preparation time 30 minutes
Cooking time 10—12 minutes
Oven temperature 450°F. Gas Mark 8
Makes 8

You will need

$\frac{1}{4}$ quantity Danish pastry (see page 130)
$\frac{1}{2}$ quantity butter filling (see page 131)
2 level teaspoons ground cinnamon
water or rum icing (see page 139)

Roll the pastry out into a rectangle approximately

A Danish pastry plait

A selection of Danish pastries

16 by 6 inches. Spread the pastry with the butter filling and scatter ground cinnamon on top. Roll up from the short end to make a fat Swiss roll shape. Cut into 8 slices and place these on a baking sheet. Leave to prove for 15 minutes. Bake in a very hot oven for 10—12 minutes. When cold decorate with water or rum icing (see recipe page 139 and photograph page 117).

WINDMILL

D. VEJRMÖLLE

Preparation time 30 minutes
Cooking time 10—12 minutes
Oven temperature 450°F. Gas Mark 8
Makes 8

You will need

¼ quantity Danish pastry (see page 130)
approximately 2 oz. almond paste (see page 131)
beaten egg
redcurrant jelly

Roll out the pastry and cut into eight 4-inch squares. Put a little of the almond paste in the centre of each. Cut from each corner to within ½ inch of the centre of each square, fold one corner of each triangular piece thus formed towards the centre and press them firmly into the almond paste (see photograph page 132). Leave on baking sheets for 15 minutes to prove, brush with beaten egg and bake in a very hot

oven for 10—12 minutes. When cool, place a little redcurrant jelly in the centre of each windmill.

SHORT PLAITS

D. STÆNGER

Preparation time 15 minutes
Cooking time 10—12 minutes
Oven temperature 450°F. Gas Mark 8
To serve 8

You will need

¼ quantity Danish pastry (see page 130) *or* trimmings from other Danish pastries
½ oz. currants
beaten egg
water icing (see page 139)

Divide the pastry into 3 equal portions and shape each into a long roll. Secure the 3 rolls together at one end and plait them together (see photograph above). Cut into 4-inch lengths and place these on a baking sheet to prove for 15 minutes. Alternatively, bake in one long plait and cut into pieces when cold. Brush the plait with the beaten egg and sprinkle it with currants. Bake in a very hot oven for 10—12 minutes. When cool, brush with water icing (see page 139).

133

PUFF PASTRY

D. SMØRDEJ (BUTTERDEJ)
N. TERTEDEIG
S. SMÖRDEG

Preparation time 30 minutes

You will need

8 oz. plain flour
approximately $\frac{1}{4}$ pint (U.S. $\frac{2}{3}$ cup) cold water
8 oz. butter, sliced

Mix the flour and water to a dough; chill for 15 minutes. Roll into a square about $\frac{1}{2}$ inch thick on a lightly floured board. Spread the butter, which should be the same consistency as the dough, over half the pastry. Fold over the other half and turn the pastry so that the folded edge is on your left hand side. Re-roll to a rectangle and fold the bottom third over and the top third over that. Chill for 15—20 minutes. Roll and fold the dough twice more in the way described above, and chill between each rolling.

Before finally shaping the pastry, it should be rolled out to the required thickness and left in a cold place for 15 minutes before being cut out. If the pastry is not allowed to rest it tends to shrink, resulting in uneven shapes when it is cut. The pastry should always be ice-cold when placed on a baking sheet, which should have been rinsed in cold water or covered with silicone paper, and it should always be baked in a very hot oven.

Puff pastry is used for a variety of cakes, but it is also used for savoury courses, patty cases, puff paste triangles or half moons usually served with elegant fish and shellfish dishes as well as meat dishes.
Note
The pastry may be prepared the day before use.

PUFF PASTRY TRIANGLES

D. BUTTERDEJSSNITTER

Preparation time 30 minutes
Cooking time 8—10 minutes
Oven temperature 450°F. Gas Mark 8
To serve 6

You will need

$\frac{1}{2}$ quantity puff pastry recipe (see above)

Roll out the pastry into a $\frac{1}{2}$-inch thick square, on a lightly floured baking table, and leave it in a cold place for 15 minutes before cutting out into triangles,

crescents or diamond shapes. Place these close together so that they do not lose their shapes during the baking. Brush with a little beaten egg and bake for 8—10 minutes until golden brown in a very hot oven.

Cool on wire trays for a minute and serve, whilst still hot, with Norwegian Fish Mousse, Creamed Shellfish or Mock Turtle (see pages 77 and 84).

DANISH BUTTER CAKE

D. SMØRKAGE

Preparation time 40 minutes
Cooking time 20—25 minutes
Oven temperature 425°F. Gas Mark 7
To serve 6—8

You will need

6 oz. plain flour
4 oz. butter, cut into small knobs
$1\frac{1}{2}$ oz. fresh yeast
1 tablespoon granulated sugar
1 whole standard egg, beaten
$\frac{1}{2}$ quantity custard cream filling
   (see page 137)
butter filling (see page 131)

Sift the flour into a large mixing bowl and rub in the butter. Stir the yeast with the sugar in a cup until it is a creamy consistency and add it, with the egg, to the flour and butter. Mix to a smooth dough. Cover with a cloth and leave to rise in a warm, but not hot, place. When it has nearly doubled its original size, turn the dough out on to a floured board and knead it for several minutes, adding more sifted flour if necessary. Roll out one-third of the dough and use to line the base of a well-greased, 9-inch cake tin (preferably with detachable sides). Spread custard cream filling over the dough. Roll out the rest of the dough into a rectangle about $\frac{1}{4}$ inch thick. Spread butter filling on this, taking care not to spread it right out to the edges. Roll up the dough as you would a Swiss roll and cut it into nine slices. Lay the slices on the custard covered dough. Put the cake in a warm place to rise for about one hour. Bake in a hot oven for about 20—25 minutes. When the cake is cold, decorate with spirals of rum icing (see recipe page 139 and photograph, page 132).

VARIATION
The cake may be baked in a 3-pint (U.S. $7\frac{1}{2}$ cup) ring mould with or without the custard (see photograph page 117).

A Danish Christmas Eve dinner table

Deep fried Christmas biscuits; brown Christmas biscuits and vanilla Christmas biscuits

MILLE-FEUILLES GÂTEAU

D. BUTTERDEJSTÆRTE
N. LAGTERTE
S. TUSENBLADSTÅRTA

Preparation time 1 hour
Cooking time 6—7 minutes
Oven temperature 450°F. Gas Mark 8
Serves 16

You will need

puff pastry (see page 134)
½—¾ pint (U.S. 1¼—1¾ cups) apple purée
custard cream filling (see recipe 2, this page)
   or ½ pint whipped cream
water, lemon or rum icing (see pages 139)

Divide the dough into 6 or 7 pieces and roll each on greaseproof paper. Leave the dough in a cold place before cutting into thin circles, 10—11 inches in diameter. Prick and brush them with cold water and sprinkle a little sugar on top. Bake the bases, on the paper, in a very hot oven until golden brown, about 6—7 minutes. Remove them from the baking sheets, but leave on the paper until ready to put the cake together. Mix the icing and spread this over the top of one of the bases. Sandwich the remainder of the circles together with apple purée and custard, or cream, between each layer and top with the iced one.

CUSTARD CREAM FILLING 1.

D. KAGECREME
N. VANILJEKREM
S. VANILJKRÄM

Preparation time 10—15 minutes
Cooking time 5 minutes

You will need

2 eggs
2 oz. sugar
2 oz. plain flour
1 pint single cream or milk
¼ vanilla pod *or*
   vanilla sugar to taste

Beat the eggs with the sugar until thick; gradually work in the flour. Bring the cream to the boil with the vanilla pod in it, remove this and pour the cream into the egg mixture and stir. Return the custard to the saucepan and let it boil gently for 2—3 minutes,

stirring all the time to prevent it sticking to the bottom of the pan. Leave the custard to cool down before using it as filling for cakes.

CUSTARD CREAM FILLING 2.

D. KAGECREME
N. VANILJEKREM
S. VANILJKRÄM

Preparation time 10—15 minutes
Cooking time 5 minutes

You will need

4 egg yolks (use standard eggs)
2 tablespoons granulated sugar
1½ level tablespoons plain flour
2 level teaspoons potato flour
¾ pint milk (U.S. 1¾ cups) or single cream
vanilla flavouring to taste
¼ pint (U.S. ⅔ cup) double cream whipped

Stir the egg yolks in a saucepan with the sugar, add the flour and potato flour, and gradually stir in the milk. Place the saucepan over medium heat and whisk the mixture until it begins to thicken. Add vanilla sugar, remove from heat and leave to cool. When custard is quite cold, fold in the whipped cream.

VARIATION

When this custard is used as a filling in layer cakes, it is sometimes made in the following way:

5 thin leaves gelatine
4 eggs
scant 2 oz. sugar
1 pint (U.S. 2½ cups) double or single cream
¼ vanilla pod

Soak the gelatine in cold water for 10 minutes. Whisk the eggs and sugar until light and frothy. Bring the cream, with the vanilla pod, to the boil; remove the pod and pour the boiling cream into the eggs. Strain, melt and stir the gelatine into the warm custard. Leave the custard to cool completely before using.

Custard Cream Tarts and Medals

CUSTARD CREAM TARTS

D. LINSER
N. LINSER

Preparation time 30 minutes
Cooking time 15—20 minutes
Oven temperature 400°F. Gas Mark 6
Makes 20
To serve 8

You will need

9 oz. plain flour
2 oz. icing sugar
7 oz. butter
2 egg yolks
custard cream filling (see page 137)

Sift the flour and the icing sugar into a bowl. Cut the cold butter into small pieces, and rub it into the flour with the fingertips, until the ingredients resemble breadcrumbs. Make a well in the middle and drop in the egg yolks. Work the pastry lightly together by the hand until blended. Wrap the pastry in waxed-paper and chill for 1 hour. Roll out two-thirds of the pastry to $\frac{1}{8}$-inch thickness and line well-buttered tartlet tins with it. Place a teaspoon of custard cream filling in each. Roll out the remaining pastry and cut out rounds to cover each tartlet tin (see photograph above). Press the edges of the pastry together. Bake in a fairly hot oven until light brown around the edge of the pastry (about 15—20 minutes). Allow to cool down in tins before removing them, as the cakes are very fragile.

One large custard cream tart can be made from the above recipe. Use a large round tin with detachable sides.

TARTS WITH RICE FILLING

D. RISKAGER

Preparation time 30 minutes
Baking time 15—20 minutes
Oven temperature 375—400°F. Gas Mark 5—6
Makes about 20 cakes

You will need

custard cream tart pastry (see this page)
1 egg
1 tablespoon sugar
5 almonds, blanched and chopped
1 teaspoon vanilla sugar
1 teacup cold rice porridge
icing sugar

Line greased, fluted, tartlet tins with the pastry and place them on a baking sheet. Stir the egg, sugar, almonds, and vanilla sugar into the rice porridge. Put some of the filling into each tin. Bake the cakes in a fairly hot oven for 15—20 minutes. Cool in the tins and when they are cold turn out carefully, and sprinkle with icing sugar.

MEDALS

D. MEDALJER

Preparation time 30 minutes
Cooking time 7—8 minutes
Oven temperature 350—375°F. Gas Mark 4—5
To serve 8

You will need

custard cream tart pastry (see opposite)
custard cream filling (see page 137)
icing
vanilla, chocolate or rum icing (see page 139)
redcurrant jelly

Roll the pastry out thinly and cut into rounds with a 2½-inch cutter. Place on a greased baking sheet and bake in a moderate to fairly hot oven for about 7—8 minutes, until golden brown. Leave to cool down completely. Spread half the baked biscuits with custard cream filling, and decorate the remaining half with vanilla, chocolate or rum icing (see page 139) and a dab of redcurrant jelly. Place the decorated biscuit on top of the custard-covered ones, to form a sandwich (see photograph page 128).

VARIATION

One large Medal may be made from the above recipe and whipped cream, plain or flavoured, may be used instead of custard cream filling.

WATER ICING

D. VANDGLASUR
N. SUKKERGLASUR
S. SOCKERGLASYR

Preparation time 5 minutes

You will need

4 oz. icing sugar
1½—2 tablespoons water

Mix the sugar and water and stir until the icing is smooth. Spread the icing with a warmed palette knife. If the icing is spread over warm cakes it will become transparent, if it is spread over cold cakes it will become opaque.
Note
For different types of icing the following ingredients may be added:

COLOURED ICINGS
Tint with a few drops of food colouring.

VANILLA ICING
Add a little vanilla flavouring. Alternatively, omit the water and add:

RUM ICING
1½ tablespoons rum

ORANGE ICING
1½ tablespoons orange juice and grated orange rind

LEMON ICING
1½ tablespoons lemon juice and grated lemon rind

MOCHA ICING
1½ tablespoons very strong black coffee.

DANISH OTHELLO LAYER CAKE

OTHELLO LAGKAGE

The Danes are particularly imaginative when it comes to naming cakes. 'Tosca Cake' and 'Othello Layer Cake' are splendid examples. The last must surely be one of the richest cakes ever concocted.

Preparation time 1½ hours
Cooking time 12—15 minutes
Oven temperature 335°F. Gas Mark 3
To serve 8—10

You will need

3 large eggs
4½ oz. granulated sugar
1 tablespoon water
2 oz. plain flour
2 oz. potato flour
1 level teaspoon baking powder
custard cream filling (see recipe 2, page 137)
macaroon cake (see page 129)
chocolate icing (optional)
whipped cream (optional)
double quantity almond paste (optional, see page 131)

Whip the eggs until thick and frothy, add sugar and water and whisk again. Sift the flour, potato flour and baking powder and fold lightly into the egg mixture; pour into 2 well-greased, 9 to 10-inch round sandwich tins. Bake in a moderate oven for approximately 12 minutes. Turn out on to a wire rack and leave to cool—but for a few minutes only. While the sponges are still warm, assemble the cake. Spread half the custard filling on to one of the sponges. Place the macaroon cake on top and spread it with the remaining custard filling. Finally, put the second sponge on top.
When the cake is cold, it may be decorated in any of the following three ways:
1. Cover the top with chocolate icing and place a strip of almond paste ¼-inch thick and as wide as the depth of the layer cake, around the sides.
2. Omit the almond paste and decorate the cake around the edge with whipped cream (see photograph page 115).
3. Cover the top with almond paste and place a strip of almond paste, ¼-inch thick and as wide as the depth of the cake, round the sides. Cut out small cornets of almond paste and place these around the top of the cake. Place a little chocolate dot into the centre of each cornet and decorate the base of the cake with whipped cream (see photograph, page 140).

Spreading filling on Othello layer cake

Decorated Othello layer cake

TOSCA CAKE

D. TOSCATÆRTE
N. TOSCAKAKE
S. TOSCATÅRTA

Preparation time 30 minutes
Cooking time 35 minutes
Oven temperature 350°F. Gas Mark 4 *then*
                400°F. Gas Mark 6
To serve 6—8

You will need

2 eggs
5 oz. sugar
1 oz. dark brown soft sugar
2 oz. melted butter
3 bitter almonds *or*
   2 teaspoons grated orange rind
5 oz. plain flour
1½ teaspoon baking powder
4 tablespoons double cream

FOR THE TOPPING
2 oz. butter
2 oz. sugar
3½ oz. almonds, blanched and coarsely
   chopped
1 tablespoon double cream
2 tablespoons plain flour

Stir the eggs and sugar until frothy and light in colour. Add the melted butter and grate the bitter almonds or rind into the mixture. Fold in the sifted flour and the baking powder, and finally, stir in the cream. Pour the mixture into a well-buttered 8 to 9-inch flan tin and bake in a moderate oven for 20 minutes. Increase the heat to 400°F. Gas Mark 6. Combine the butter, sugar, almonds, cream and flour in a saucepan with a heavy base over medium heat. Let the mixture reach boiling point and then withdraw it from the heat. Spread the almond mixture over the top of the cake, return it to a fairly hot oven and bake for approximately 15 minutes more or until the top is golden brown.

CHOCOLATE ICING

D. CHOKOLADEGLASUR
N. SJOKOLADEGLASUR
S. CHOKLADGLASYR

Preparation time 5—10 minutes

You will need

3½ oz. plain block chocolate
1 tablespoon tepid water
4 oz. icing sugar
3 tablespoons water or strong coffee

Grate the chocolate or break it up into small pieces. Melt it with the water in a double saucepan over low heat. Stir the sugar with the water or coffee in a bowl until smooth and add the melted chocolate.

Note

Chocolate icing may be made simply by melting chocolate without any additional ingredients. Melt the chocolate over very low heat in a double saucepan or a small basin over a pan of hot water. Cover the container, as it is important that neither water nor steam should come in contact with the chocolate, since this would make it dull and granular. The chocolate becomes glossier and easier to handle if a little unsalted butter or coconut butter is stirred in; allow 1 tablespoon to 3½ oz. chocolate. Chocolate flakes for decorating cakes and sweets may be made from melted chocolate as described above. Pour the melted chocolate onto a clean baking sheet and allow to set. Scrape it off the baking sheet with a long, sharp knife, so that the chocolate rolls up into long curly flakes.

Tosca Cake

CHOCOLATE CAKE

D. CHOKOLADEKAGE

This rich chocolate cake is an old family recipe which should not be spoiled by having any icing put on it. It is delicious served with chilled whipped cream, though this is not strictly necessary either.

Preparation time 20—25 minutes
Cooking time 1 hour
Oven temperature 375°F. Gas Mark 5
To serve 8—10

You will need

8 oz. butter
8 oz. granulated sugar
4 large eggs
6½ oz. dark, cooking chocolate
a little strong coffee
8 oz. plain flour
1 level teaspoon baking powder

Cream the butter and sugar. Add the eggs, one at a time, beating the mixture well after each one. Melt the chocolate with a little coffee over low heat—do not allow it to boil. Stir the chocolate into the creamed mixture. Finally, fold in the sifted flour and baking powder. Pour the mixture into a well-greased, 2 lb. loaf tin and bake for approximately 1 hour, towards the top of a fairly hot oven.
Note
If the cake is getting too dark on top after 50 minutes' baking, cover it with a piece of buttered greaseproof paper.

CARDAMOM CAKE

D. KARDEMOMMEKAGE
N. KARDEMOMMEKAKE
S. KARDEMUMMAKAKA

Preparation time 15 minutes
Cooking time 50 minutes
Oven temperature 375°F. Gas Mark 5
To serve 8—10

You will need

9 oz. butter
9 oz. sugar
3 eggs
13½ oz. plain flour
3 teaspoons baking powder
10 seeds of cardamom, crushed and ground
¼ pint (U.S. ⅔ cup) milk
3 tablespoons raisins
3 tablespoons cut, mixed peel
½ oz. blanched, slivered almonds

Cream the butter and sugar. Add the eggs, one at a time, beating the mixture well after each one. Fold in the sifted flour, baking powder and the ground cardamom. Stir in the milk a little at a time, and add the raisins, mixed peel and almonds. Pour the cake mixture into a well-greased oblong 2 lb. loaf tin and bake for about 50 minutes in a fairly hot oven.

MAZARINS

D. MAZARINER
N. MAZARINER
S. MAZARINER

Preparation time 30 minutes
Cooking time 20 minutes
Oven temperature 375—400°F. Gas Mark 5—6
Makes 12

You will need

3½ oz. almonds
2½ oz. butter
3 oz. icing sugar
2 small eggs
a little green food colouring
½ quantity Custard Cream Tart pastry (see
    page 138)
chocolate icing or icing sugar

Blanch and grind the almonds for the filling. Cream
the butter and sugar until smooth and add the eggs
one at a time. Fold in the almonds and stir in a drop
of green food colouring. Line greased, fluted
tartlet tins with the pastry and place them on a baking sheet. Put filling into each tin and bake in a
moderate to fairly hot oven for about 20 minutes.
Turn out the tartlets when they are cool. Decorate
with either chocolate icing (see page 140) or sifted
icing sugar (see photograph page 128).
The same quantities may be used for an 8-inch flan
tin. Allow about 35—40 minutes baking time.

APPLE CAKE WITH CINNAMON

D. ÆBLEKAGE MED KANEL

Preparation time 30 minutes
Cooking time 35 minutes
Oven temperature 355°F. Gas Mark 4
To serve 4—6

You will need

5½ oz. butter
5½ oz. granulated sugar
2 large eggs
5½ oz. plain flour
1 level teaspoon baking powder
2—3 large cooking apples
1 oz. almonds, blanched and chopped
2 tablespoons sugar, mixed with ground
    cinnamon to taste
1 tablespoon coffee crystals

Cream the butter and sugar. Add the eggs, one
at a time, beating the mixture well after each
addition. Fold in the sifted flour and baking powder.
Peel, core and slice the apples. Place half the cake
mixture into a shallow, hinged, 10-inch cake tin:
spread the cake mixture with a palette knife, and do
not be alarmed if the mixture seems rather stiff.
Arrange the sliced apples in overlapping layers on
top of the cake mixture; sprinkle with chopped
almonds, sugar and ground cinnamon. Spread the
remaining half of the cake mixture on top. Sprinkle
with coffee crystals and bake for about 35 minutes
in a moderate oven. Serve lukewarm with chilled
whipped cream.

MARZIPAN CAKES

D. KRANSEKAGER

Preparation time 30 minutes
Cooking time 15—20 minutes
Oven temperature 300°F. Gas Mark 2
To serve 4—6

You will need

1 lb. ground almonds
4 oz. icing sugar
4 oz. castor sugar
2 tablespoons water
3 egg whites

FOR THE ICING
4½ oz. icing sugar
1 egg white
½ teaspoon vinegar

Mix all the ingredients and heat in a saucepan over
low heat, until the almond paste is slightly roasted
and has absorbed all the liquid. Remove the saucepan from the heat and leave the almond paste to
cool competely. Roll it out into strips, the thickness
of a finger and the length of a baking sheet. Place the
strips on a well-greased baking sheet, which has
been lightly sprinkled with flour. Pinch each strip
with thumb and forefinger with an upward move-
ment, so that the strips are broad at the base and
slope off to a sharp ridge on top. Cut into 2—3 inch
lengths, and bake in a cool oven for about 15—20
minutes, until the cakes are light brown on top only.
When the cakes are cold prepare the icing.
Sift the icing sugar, stir in the egg white and the
vinegar and keep stirring until the mixture is of an
even consistency. Decorate cakes with thin zig-zag
lines of white icing (see photograph page 115).

ALMOND MUSSELS

S. MANDELFORMAR

Preparation time 35—40 minutes
Cooking time   30 minutes
Oven temperature 350—400°F. Gas Mark 4—6
Makes about   40—50 cakes

You will need

3½ oz. almonds, blanched and ground
2—3 bitter almonds, blanched and ground
8 oz. plain flour
4½ oz. sugar
5 oz. butter
1 egg yolk

Chop the fat into the flour and sugar and add the almonds and the egg yolk. Work to a dough. Leave it in a cold place for 30 minutes. Roll it out into a sausage-shaped strip and cut it into equal pieces. Put these into greased fluted patty tins and press out each piece of the dough with the thumb so that it is thicker towards the edges than it is towards the base. Put the tins on to a baking sheet and bake in a moderate to fairly hot oven for 10—12 minutes. Remove the tins and leave the cakes to cool down before turning them out. The almond mussels may be filled with whipped cream or custard cream filling (see page 137) and fresh or bottled fruit (see photograph, page 128).

POPPINS

D. TEBIRKES

Preparation time 20—25 minutes
Cooking time   10—15 minutes
Oven temperature 425°F. Gas Mark 7
Makes   8

You will need

9 oz. plain flour
¼ teaspoon salt
2 teaspoons sugar
4 fl. oz. (U.S. ½ cup) milk
1 oz. fresh yeast
2¾ oz. cold, unsalted butter, cut into thin slices
1 beaten egg
poppy seeds

Sift the flour into a large mixing bowl and add the salt and sugar. Bring half the milk to boiling point and add it to the remainder of the cold milk.

Dissolve the yeast in the tepid milk and stir it until smooth before adding it to the flour. Knead the dough for a few minutes until it is smooth and puffy, cover the basin with a cloth and put it in a warm, but not hot, place for about 20—30 minutes until the dough has risen and practically doubled its size. Turn the dough on to a lightly floured board and knead it lightly for a minute, sprinkling it with a little more flour if the dough is sticky. Roll out the dough to a rectangle measuring 8 by 16 inches and place the cold sliced butter on half of it. Fold the other half of the dough over the butter. Roll out the dough again and fold it in three in both directions (first from end to end and then from side to side). Re-roll the dough into a rectangle and repeat this process once more. Finally, roll out the dough to a rectangle measuring 10 by 20 inches. Fold it in three, to make a thin strip 20 inches long, and cut this into 8 pieces. Place the pieces on a well-greased baking sheet, cover with a cloth and leave to rise for 10—15 minutes. Brush with beaten egg and scatter plenty of poppy seeds over the top. Bake in a hot oven for 10—15 minutes. Tap the poppins on their bases. If they sound hollow they are cooked.

Poppins

Danish Lenten pretzels

Pastry shells, filled with creamed mushrooms

Baked pastry shells

DANISH LENTEN PRETZELS

D. KOMMENSKRINGLER

Preparation time 30 minutes
Cooking time 15 minutes
Oven temperature 425°F. Gas Mark 7
To serve 12

You will need

1 lb. 2 oz. plain flour
1 teaspoon salt
1 oz. sugar
approximately ½ pint (U.S. 1¼ cups) milk
1 oz. fresh yeast
3½ oz. butter
beaten egg or milk
½ oz. caraway seeds

Sift the flour with the salt and sugar. Heat half the milk to boiling point, remove from heat and add to the rest of the milk. Cream the yeast with a little of the tepid milk and allow the butter to melt in the remainder. Add this, together with the creamed yeast, to the flour. Knead well. Leave the dough in a warm, but not hot place, to rise until it has about doubled its size. Divide into 12 portions and roll these out into long sausage shapes measuring about 12—15 inches long. Twist each piece of dough into overlapping loops (see photograph, page 143).
Place the pretzels on well-greased baking sheets and leave to rise for 10—15 minutes. Brush with beaten egg and sprinkle with caraway seeds. Bake in a hot oven for 12—15 minutes until they are light brown.
Note
The pretzels are sometimes cooked by first lowering them into boiling water. As soon as they float to the surface they are removed with a slotted spoon, brushed with beaten egg and sprinkled with caraway seeds before being baked as above.

PASTRY SHELLS

D. SKALLER
N. SKJELL
S. SNÄCKOR

These pastry shells can be made in advance and stored in air-tight tins until ready for use with either savoury or sweet fillings. They look attractive when baked on the backs of real scallop shells, but fluted tartlet tins may be used instead. They are useful for serving left-overs or for hors d'oeuvre.

Preparation time 30 minutes
Cooking time 10—12 minutes
Oven temperature 425°F. Gas Mark 7
Makes about 12

You will need

4½ oz. plain flour
pinch salt
3 oz. butter
1 standard egg
1 tablespoon single cream

Sift the flour and salt into a basin; cut the butter into small pieces into the flour and rub it in. Add the egg and cream and mix together lightly to make a soft dough. Put the dough in a cold place for 1—2 hours, or until it is cold and firm enough to roll out. Turn it onto a floured board and roll out thinly (⅛ inch thick). Cut the pastry around the scallop shells or individual fluted tartlet tins. Grease the backs of the shells or tins and cover with the pastry dough. Place on baking sheets and bake in a hot oven for 10—12 minutes, or until golden. Leave to cool before removing from the shells or tins. Serve with a savoury filling such as creamed mushrooms, creamed sweetbreads or creamed shellfish (see pages 110, 94 and 77). The shells can also be used for sweet fillings like fresh cream or, alternatively, custard cream filling with fresh or canned fruit.

ALMOND SNAPS

D. MANDELSPÅNER
N. MANDELFLARN
S. MANDELFLARN

Preparation time 25 minutes
Cooking time 7—8 minutes
Oven temperature 350—375°F. Gas Mark 4—5
Makes about 30

You will need

3½ oz. almonds
3½ oz. butter
3 oz. sugar
1 tablespoon plain flour
2 tablespoons milk

Blanch and shred the almonds. Mix them with the butter, sugar, flour and milk and heat gently only till the fat melts. Put well spaced spoonsful of the mixture on to greased and floured baking sheets. Bake for about 7—8 minutes in a moderate to fairly hot oven until the cakes are light brown. Remove the baking sheet from the oven and let the cakes cook for half a minute before removing them with a sharp thin knife. Place the cakes over a rolling pin or a round tube to shape into curled snaps while the cakes are still warm.

VARIATION

Prepare almond snaps as above, but do not shape them into curls. Leave them to cool down completely before brushing the bases with melted plain chocolate. Leave them to set on greaseproof paper with the chocolate side uppermost.

DEEP FRIED CHRISTMAS BISCUITS

D. KLEJNER
N. FATTIGMANN
S. KLENÄTER

Preparation time 30—40 minutes
Cooking time 3—4 minutes each biscuit
Makes about 80

You will need

9 oz. plain flour
1 teaspoon ground cardamom
4½ oz. butter
2½ oz. granulated sugar
2 tablespoons double cream
2 teaspoons brandy
1 large egg
icing sugar
fat for deep frying

Sift the flour with the cardamom. Cut up the butter into small pieces and rub into the flour, add the sugar, cream, brandy and egg and knead well. Leave the dough in a cool place for 1 hour. Roll out on a lightly floured board to ¼ inch thickness and cut into 1-inch strips with a pastry cutter. Cut these strips into 4-inch pieces and with the pastry cutter or the point of a sharp knife slit the middle of each strip (see photograph below). Pull one end of the strip through the slit to make a half-bow. Fry in deep fat for 3—4 minutes until biscuits are light brown. Drain on absorbent paper. When biscuits are cold serve sprinkled with icing sugar.

Shaping deep fried Christmas biscuits

Lifting deep fried Christmas biscuits out of the oil

VANILLA CHRISTMAS BISCUITS

D. VANILLEKRANSE
N. VANILJEKRANSER
S. SPRITSAR

This is a basic dough used for many different biscuits flavoured and shaped in various ways. The first variation is known as Finnish Bread, the second as Jewish Cakes.

Preparation time 25 minutes
Cooking time 30 minutes
Oven temperature 400°F. Gas Mark 6
Makes about 70

You will need

10½ oz. plain flour
2½ oz. granulated sugar
4—5 bitter almonds, grated, *or*
   2 oz. blanched almonds, finely chopped
½ vanilla pod
7 oz. butter
1 egg yolk

Mix the flour, sugar and almonds together directly on to the baking table. Split the half vanilla pod and scrape the seeds into the mixture; chop in the butter and add the egg yolk. Work the dough together. Pipe the dough into long strips and cut these into pieces about 4 inches long. Shape these into rings and place on greased baking sheets. Bake in a fairly hot oven for 8—10 minutes, until the biscuits turn light golden.

VARIATIONS

1. Omit the almonds and vanilla. Put the dough in a cold place for about 1 hour. Divide the dough into 8 portions and roll these into strips 12 inches long; place them close together and brush with lightly beaten egg. Cut the lengths all at the same time, into 2-inch pieces and dip these in sugar and chopped almonds. Place on greased baking sheets and bake as Vanilla biscuits above.
2. Omit almonds and vanilla. Put the dough in a cold place for about 1 hour. Roll out the dough into ⅛-inch thickness and cut out with a 2-inch round cutter. Brush the biscuits with beaten egg and sprinkle with cinnamon and coarse sugar crystals. Place on baking sheets and bake as vanilla biscuits (see photograph page 136).

BROWN CHRISTMAS BISCUITS

D. BRUNE KAGER
N. BRUNE KAKER or
   PEPPERKAKER
S. PEPPARKAKOR

Preparation time 30—40 minutes
Cooking time 8—10 minutes
Oven temperature 375°F. Gas Mark 5

You will need

4½ oz. butter
4½ oz. granulated sugar
3½ oz. golden syrup
1 oz. almonds, blanched and coarsely chopped
½ oz. grated lemon rind
½ oz. cut mixed peel
9 oz. plain flour
1 level teaspoon baking powder
2 level teaspoons ground cloves
1½ level teaspoons ground ginger
2 tablespoons ground cinnamon
½ oz. flaked almonds

Heat the butter, sugar and syrup in a saucepan, but do not let it boil. Remove the saucepan from the heat and allow to cool a little. Stir in the almonds, lemon rind and mixed peel. Sift the flour, baking powder, cloves, ginger and cinnamon; add to the mixture and knead well. Leave the dough in a cold place until firm—overnight if convenient. Roll out the dough thinly on a lightly floured board and cut into rounds about 2 inches in diameter. Decorate each biscuit with a flaked almond and place on a well-greased sheet. Bake for about 8—10 minutes in a fairly hot oven (see photograph page 136).

GLOSSARY

Below is a list of various ingredients and foods which are useful to have in store, when cooking the Scandinavian way. Some may be entirely novel and others may have familiar names although they are not standard items in an average larder or cupboard.

Cardamom—is obtainable at chemists and most big stores. Usually sold as seeds, but sometimes already ground: the former is the most potently flavoured and therefore the best. Cardamom is used extensively in Scandinavian baking—in Indian cooking it belongs in the curries!

Vanilla pods—are obtainable at chemists and most big stores. They should be stored before and after use in sugar, providing vanilla sugar for baking as well.

Almonds—Scandinavian cakes and puddings are rich in almonds, whole and ground. Bitter almonds are sometimes hard to come by—unless you grow them yourself—but these are often used sparingly with the sweet variety for a good sharp almond flavouring.

Leaf gelatine—is so much nicer and easier to use than the powdered type which always seems so 'gluey'. 5 sheets of *fine* gelatine is equal to ½ oz. or 3 level teaspoons powdered gelatine. Continental leaf gelatine tends to be the *fine* variety but some other kinds are thicker in which case use half the amount (i.e. 2½ leaves). This amount of gelatine will set approximately 1 pint liquid in the refrigerator.

Fresh yeast—always gives much nicer and more reliable results than dried yeast. Keep yeast pressed into a bowl standing upside down in a saucer with a little cold water. Store in a cool place—either in the refrigerator or in a cold larder. Fresh yeast will keep for 3—4 weeks like this.

Vinegar—tarragon, red or white wine vinegar should be used, but not malt vinegar, which has far too penetrating a flavour for most purposes.

Potato flour—is used for thickening in the same way as you would use cornflour, but don't let it boil, or it will make the mixture stringy. Potato flour is also used a great deal in baking for very light sponges. Do not confuse potato flour with instant potato powder.

Curry powder—should be discreetly used in soups, sauces and salads.

Danish ryebread—is ideal for Danish open sandwiches. It is dark brown, rather close-textured bread, and is usually sold sliced in packets of 14 slices. Don't confuse this with the rye bread sold in continental delicatessen shops, which is an off-white bread with caraway seeds.

Norwegian flatbröd—is as thin as wafers and looks deceptively as if it would not have much flavour. It keeps well and is delicious.

Swedish crisp bread (Knäckebröd)—keeps well and is delicious.

Redcurrant jelly—is used with all game dishes and also as one of the ingredients of game sauce.

Rose hips—are used fresh or dried for soup.

Lingonberries (wild cranberries)—are used with both savoury and sweet dishes.

Pickled gherkins—are sweet-sour. They are easy to pickle yourself, but are obtainable from most stores.

Poppy seeds and caraway seeds—are used to scatter on top of home-made bread and rolls.

Dried prunes—used for both savoury and sweet dishes.

Canned Matjes herrings or Gaffelbiter—are one of the commonest features of the Smörgåsbord.

Parsley—can be stored, after cleaning, in plastic bags in a deep freeze or it can be kept for a very long time if it is chopped and packed in glass jars with layers of salt, or, of course, grown in a pot on the window-sill or in the open ground. Don't put parsley into a dish which may be *reheated* the following day—this is potentially a source of food poisoning. It may therefore be safer to serve parsley separately.

Dill—is probably the most popular herb in Scandinavian cooking. An annual herb sown in April and used in partically all herring dishes as well as in many others, it can be used dried as well. The leaves are used during the early summer, either in sprigs or chopped. The crown of the dill is used for pickling gherkins etc. Fennel is the only other herb which resembles dill, but it has a stronger flavour.

Chives—are another great favourite with Scandinavian cooks. They are perennial and easily grown in pots or in the open. Green tops of spring onions may be used, but are much stronger than chives.

Horseradish—is a weed! Grow it in a confined space so that it won't ruin your garden. Otherwise buy it at great expense from the greengrocer, who will tell you it is usually imported from France! It has a delightfully sharp flavour when freshly grated, but it loses its whiteness quickly and becomes an ugly blue-black colour unless it is covered up. Use it in sauces and salads. Freshly grated on Danish open sandwiches is a characteristic way of using it.

INDEX

ACKNOWLEDGEMENTS

These colour photographs are by the courtesy of:

DANISH FOOD CENTRE

Danish open sandwiches	page 39
A typical after-theatre supper	page 40
Christmas biscuits	page 136

*The following pictures first appeared in
'Armchair Visit to Denmark' and
are reproduced here by kind permission of:*

**THE FEDERATION OF DANISH DAIRY
ASSOCIATIONS** and **DANISH FOOD
CENTRE**

A Danish Christmas Eve dinner table	page 135
The smörgåsbord	page 19
Poached cod	page 76
Roast beef with glazed onions	page 98

PLUMROSE LIMITED

Smoked buckling omelette and fried pork and apples	page 85
Danish chervil soup and pancakes	page 58

Asparagus in pickled salmon
and meat rissoles	page 87
Spring chicken with cream gravy	page 97

Black and white photographs by courtesy of:

BROWN AND POLSON LIMITED

A Swedish smörgåsbord	page 15
A Norwegian smörgåsbord	page 12

DANISH FOOD CENTRE

Glazed gammon, Danish cheeses and layer cake	page 78
Rolled veal sausage	page 31
A selection of Danish open sandwiches	page 34
A typical Danish lunch	page 48
Pork omelette	page 53
Burning passion	page 83
A selection of Danish cheeses	page 111
Fish soufflé	page 50
Danish Lenten pretzels	page 143

BIRDS EYE KITCHEN

Chilled Buttermilk soup	page 65